SEEING THE GLORY

A Journey into the Mystical Realm

Ian Carroll

Building Contenders
Oak Park, Il, 60304 USA
ian@buildingcontenders.com
www.buikdigcontenders.com

Printed in the United States of America

ISBN Ebook – 978-0-9982644-7-9
ISBN Paperback – 978-0-9982644-6-2

YES, *FEAST ON ALL THE TREASURES OF THE HEAVENLY REALM* AND FILL YOUR THOUGHTS WITH HEAVENLY REALITIES, AND NOT WITH THE DISTRACTIONS OF THE NATURAL REALM.

—Colossians 3:2 TPT

TABLE OF CONTENTS

ACKNOWLEDG-MENTS

I stand on the shoulder of giants, men and women of God who have pioneered in the face of criticism and rejection. To all of them, I say thank you.

I am a better man, a better child of God because of my wife Rachel. We have been happily married since March 1989. She is simply my favorite person on the planet. She is my sweetheart and my best friend.

I dedicate this book and my life to her. She has stood by me in my worst days and laughed with me on my best.

I know no one who is more passionate for the Holy Spirit than she; she truly is a friend of God and is my biggest inspiration.

I am proud to be recognized as her husband.

PROLOGUE

The mystical realm.
The unseen realm.
The quantum realm.

These are all different names for one realm—and we *all* have access to it. Sadly, many in the Church have been trained out of this realm to the point that we are often afraid of it. But Jesus is the heart of this realm—the very reason for it. So right here at the outset, remember: the heart of this realm is Jesus, and Jesus is Love.

I have been trying to write a book about the mystical realm for years. The problem is: I keep learning something new—or something different—that makes me want to start over.

In a way, we should always have that problem, right? God is unchanging, but our understanding of Him is continually expanding. I am so glad that my belief has grown since I first encountered Him, and I hope that it will continue to change and deepen.

My early Christian years were spent in a fellowship of misfits in Belfast, Northern Ireland. In this group were former drug addicts, paramilitaries, and hippies—all sold out to Jesus. I was one of the youngest at 15 years old—a brand new believer surrounded by people with more life experience and not all of it good. For the most part, we were all first-generation converts with little or no background in Christianity.

Our fellowship, Agape Fellowship, met several times a week in a house on Everton Drive in East Belfast, Northern Ireland. There an evangelist named Robert taught; He's a man to whom I owe an eternal debt of gratitude. The meetings were pretty raw and sometimes, if the Bible study went for more than an hour, there would be a break. We would never have called it a smoke break, but that's what we used it for—a group of us huddled at the side of the house where we met, having a smoke and talking about Jesus.

Scripture and evangelism became my diet. We would travel to various churches and missions around the city on Sunday nights, preaching the gospel, singing our songs, and telling testimonies of how God had saved us. I loved it. I was an itinerant preacher before I even knew such a thing existed.

At the same time, other fellowships in Belfast were being impacted by the charismatic movement. We thought those people were flaky and emotional and not doing any good for the unsaved. Although not strictly cessationist, we weren't far away. "Don't ask, don't seek" was the name of our game when it came to the Holy Spirit and His gifts.

Yet it was in this environment that my spirit eyes began to open. I vividly remember entering the meeting room of the house on Everton Drive one day. My first thought was, "Hey, the room is filled with steam." But this was weird steam. It didn't rise to the ceiling; it hung throughout the room from floor to ceiling and stayed put, even when a breeze blew through the door. My second thought was "Maybe I need glasses?"

I ignored the steam and stuffed it into a file in my mind labeled "Things I Won't Talk About." I didn't know it then, but I was going to be stuffing a lot of things into that file, including seeing angels.

I'll share some of those stories later in this book, but I should note that I've been ashamed and embarrassed of being able to see the mystical realm. For so long, the Church mistrusted any expression of the Spirit that could be classified as weird or kooky; it wasn't as attractive as it currently is in the charismatic world. In the past, whenever I shared a "weird" experience, I'd be held at arm's length. So I lived in denial.

About eight years ago, I first taught on the mystical realm in my own church, and I prefaced my teaching by saying, "I don't want to be known as the 'angel guy.'" Then, for a couple of years, I would become covered in glitter while I was preaching. I became known as "glitter boy." Truthfully? I'd prefer to be known as "angel guy"! Maybe the Holy Spirit wanted me to lift the restriction I'd put on His expression. I don't know. These days, I *do* know that I'll take everything heaven wants to dish out. I may not always be an enthusiastic seer, but I'm finally embracing what God wants me to see.

My goal for this book is to remind us that God made both the heavens and earth and designed them to function together: the unseen and the seen together. Jesus said He only did what He *saw* the Father doing. If we are to be like Him, then we too need to *see* what the Father is doing. Like Jesus, we have been given the opportunity to *see* what heaven is up to, and God is ready to massively expand this ability throughout the Church. Let's be ready.

What would you do if you knew you had access to seeing in the spirit? What actions would you take to learn and train and grow? How would you like to experience heaven coming to earth?

This reluctant seer invites you to see the unseen and to engage the mystical realm around us.

INTRODUCTION

This might sound strange, but I have long disliked the term "seer." I don't like the specialness the word has implied, and yes, I still use it simply because I can't think of a better word. My goal is to normalize the word "seer" and activate it in our everyday lives as Christians.

Scripture is filled with descriptions of the mystical realm—trances, dreams, visions, people being transported, etc. These are all spiritual realities that have an effect on the physical world. If we attach some special meaning to being a seer, we make it seem like the skill of a super-Christian instead of being part of every Christian's identity.

That specialness associated with being seers likely originates with old covenant thinking, when the presence of God was fleeting, the veil remained in place, and access to the mystical realm was reserved for "specially" gifted individuals. In the new covenant, the veil is torn, and the mystical unseen realm should be our normal. But the lack of solid teaching and understanding has complicated things. The goal has always been to see His Glory that is present in what I call our 'fused reality' of the heavens and the earth. His Glory is present, we just need, as Habakkuk 2:14 states, the knowledge of it.

Not too long ago, the prophetic was scary to the average pastor. What do you do when an intense, often "strange" person claims a direct line to the Head Office in heaven and starts telling you what God is saying? Add to that the teachings that confused prophetic utterances, the gift of prophecy, and the office of the prophet, and it is no wonder that churches kept the prophetic at arm's length. Thankfully, the prophetic gift and practice have come a long way.

When it comes to "seeing," we're kind of where the misunderstood prophetic was in the past. Church leaders often have no idea what to do with the seer ability, not to mention the often "strange" bunch of people who claim to see and engage with the mystical realm.

So what do we do?

We cultivate and train healthy seers. So I guess I'm going to have to get comfortable with that label. In fact, I won't mind it so much if we can remember that we are *all* supposed to be seers. To do that, let's embrace the fact that God has removed the barrier between heaven and earth, between the seen and unseen realm. Let's train our sight to advance the Kingdom.

WHAT IS A SEER?

After healing the crippled man at the pool of Bethesda, Jesus was accused of breaking the law and claiming He was equal with God. He responded:

> "Truly, truly, I say to you, the Son can do nothing of Himself, unless it is something He sees the Father doing; for whatever the Father does, these things the Son also does in like manner" (John 5:19 NASB).

The word here for "sees" is *blepo* which means both to see with our physical eyes and also to see with the mind's eye—to perceive. It helps to think of this perception as insight: the ability to discern the truth. It's like receiving an interpretation simultaneously with a revelation.

So, when Jesus says He only does what He *sees* the Father doing, he is saying that He has insight; he understands and discerns what is happening. If we want to do what Jesus did, we need to see what the Father is doing—either with our natural eyes, our mind's eye, or both.

THE WORLD WANTS TO SEE

Over eight billion dollars. That's how much money the *Harry Potter* franchise has brought into the movie studios, and the number continues to grow.

In the last decade, 167 movies have been made just about ghosts. And then there are the productions on Netflix, Hulu, Apple, Disney+, and other online streaming platforms. At the top of their most-viewed lists? Shows about the paranormal and supernatural.

There's the Marvel franchise. Dr. Strange. And the most popular Halloween costume for families of five continues to be the super suits from *The Incredibles*, an animated feature about a family of superheroes.

Everybody wants to be special.

You can read that either with a tone of cynicism or with a tone of excitement. Let's go with excitement; there is an opportunity here! The hunger for superheroes reveals a hunger for the supernatural—for the one, great Hero.

I think the world is bored with Christianity as we have been presenting it. They want the very things that the Church has been afraid of embracing.

For eight months, once a month, I stayed at a hotel while teaching at our School of Emerging Apostles. I was in the bar, chatting to the bartender.

The bartender asked, "So is your seminar all finished?"

And I said, "Yeah, everybody left, and I leave tomorrow."

He said, "In the fourteen years I've worked here, I've never met a group that shifts the atmosphere in this hotel like your group does. The level of spirituality and quest that your guys have is just amazing."

His words, not mine. That's pretty genuine. Does he know Jesus? I don't think so. Is he sensing and recognizing and possibly even seeing stuff in the spirit realm that's in our school? You better believe that he is.

Many people outside the Church believe in the spirit realm, but many people in the church get their panties in a bunch the minute we talk about it because they are afraid of being deceived.

You might have heard the saying: "If you take the Holy Spirit away from the church, you better make sure your coffee is good because you're gonna need something to attract people." Removing the supernatural from the Church is ridiculous. Have we read the Bible? We should be the most supernatural, mystical people on the face of the planet!

In fact, did you know that right this minute you are having an out-of-body experience? How, you might ask? You are seated with Christ in heavenly places:

> Therefore if you have been raised up with Christ, keep seeking the things above, where Christ is, seated at the right hand of God (Colossians 3:1-2 NASB).

We are currently—this minute—seated with Christ in heavenly places. And if we are not aware of that, we should be.

Like I said in the prologue, if any of this freaks you out, remember: it's all about keeping Jesus the center of everything. His story is one of the most mystical in history: immaculate conception, miracles, resurrection. Mystical mysteries for sure. If we are to do what Jesus is doing—which is what he sees the Father doing—then shouldn't we be activating our seer ability? Shouldn't that be our normal?

Normalizing the mystical, heavenly realm is vital if we are to partner with God and activate that realm here on earth. I believe God is highlighting this ability in His Church right now. I believe our worship will be more glorious, our prayer lives will be more accelerated, our spiritual warfare will be more victorious, and cities and nations will see more of God's plans for them.

However, we have some work to do. We must see ourselves as seers and act on that identity. For that reason, this book is divided into two parts: normalizing and activating the mystical realm—with the essential thread of discernment throughout. As you read, ask God for insight. Ask Him what He's up to. Ask to see.

Let's do what Jesus did. Let's see what the Father is doing.

PART ONE

NORMALIZING THE MYSTICAL REALM

1: WHAT'S YOUR "SETTING"?

Tell someone you are a seer, and they will want to know what you see. I often have no idea how to answer. Perhaps the Apostle John experienced a similar problem when he tried to describe things he saw. Take this passage for example:

> The appearance of the locusts was *like* horses prepared for battle; and on their heads *appeared* to be crowns like gold, and their faces were *like* the faces of men. They had hair *like* the hair of women, and their teeth were *like* [the teeth] of lions. They had breastplates *like* breastplates of iron; and the sound of their wings was *like* the sound of chariots, of many horses rushing to battle (Revelation 9:7-10, NASB).

Let's break it down:

- Locusts *appeared* like horses prepared for battle
- They were wearing what *appeared* to be crowns of gold
- They had faces *like* the faces of men
- They had hair *like* the hair of women
- They had teeth *like* lions or lions teeth

You get the picture. A thing seen in the mystical realm frequently appears or is like things seen on earth…but it is *not* those things. Mystical things are usually entirely different from earthly things, but we understand earthly things, so seers interpret the unseen into familiar language and images so that others can comprehend it. Scripture is full of people receiving really, really strange revelation from the mystical realm and trying to explain it to people. Don't worry; there's a biblical precedent for all of this.

Before I go on, I want to reiterate that it took me years to admit to seeing stuff, let alone to teach on it. I'm a practical, tactical guy. I was a cop in Belfast. Maybe it's God's sense of humor to ask me to write and teach about being a seer, or maybe it's because He knows that I understand the skepticism that can arise. Either way, as you keep reading, remember that Christ is at the center of all of this.

I take ministry groups to Northern Ireland, and in 2018 we drove out to visit an ancient healing well. While there, I saw a dragon on an outcrop. If I say "dragon", you know what I mean, right? But why? Why do people across time and across the world know what dragons look like? Did they ever exist? Were they actually dinosaurs? Or are they things of the spirit realm seen enough that we have a common understanding of them?

Just the other day, I had an encounter with one of my angels. He communicated to me that a ministry friend, someone I love and respect, needed help. So I texted my friend, "Why am I praying for you right now?" He immediately texted back that he and his family were under some serious spiritual attack. I prayed. Later that day, I asked my angel a little about what was going on, and he told me that help was being sent to this guy and his family and that they were about to see small victories that would precede a larger victory.

During that communication with my angel, I also sensed something else going on. Just a sense: I didn't hear or see it. I sensed that my angel and my friend's angel had known each other for a long time and had actually been part of the Jesus Movement of the 70s and 80s. This sounds weird, I know. Sensing or seeing it feels weird too. All of this can be confusing, but I want to grow my gift of sight, so I keep inviting the Holy Spirit to teach me, and I keep pressing in to Him to learn.

I have a constant awareness of the spiritual realm unless I totally switch it off, which I can. It is also possible to switch off the physical realm like Peter did; he was so connected to the mystical realm that he simply fell into trances. Even Paul himself was not immune to such deep experiences when he announced that he did not know if he was in his body or out of his body when he went to heaven.

Many people who have been labeled mentally ill experience a lot more of the mystical realm than of the physical realm. And there are plenty of Christians who behave like the physical realm has little or no meaning.

I want to suggest that both the spiritual realm and the physical realm are vitally important to live a full, abundant life in the Spirit.

I like to illustrate this with a pair of dimmer switches.

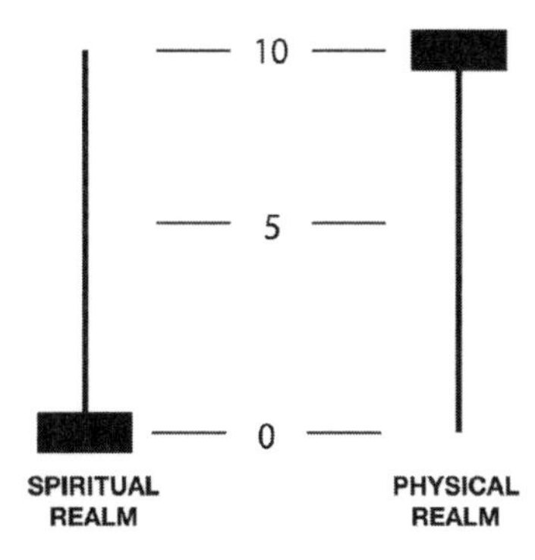

Most people do life with the dimmer switch of their mystical awareness set to zero, or pretty close to it, and their dimmer switch for the physical realm way set at ten. The spiritual realm dimmer switch frequently bounces a little off of zero during amazing worship services or at times when the prophetic is being released.

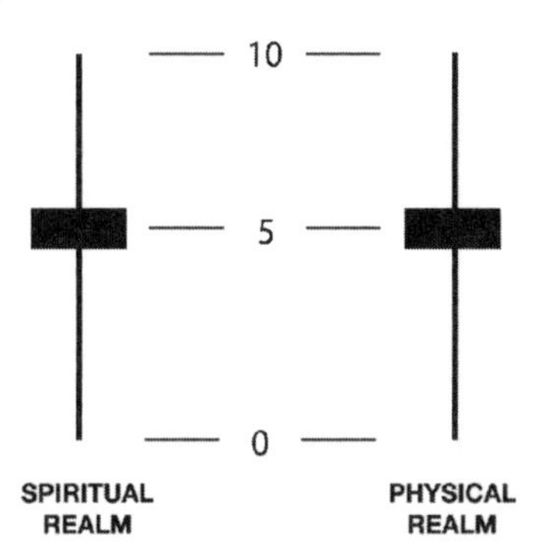

Others strive to find their balance, giving equal attention to both and end up feeling frustrated.

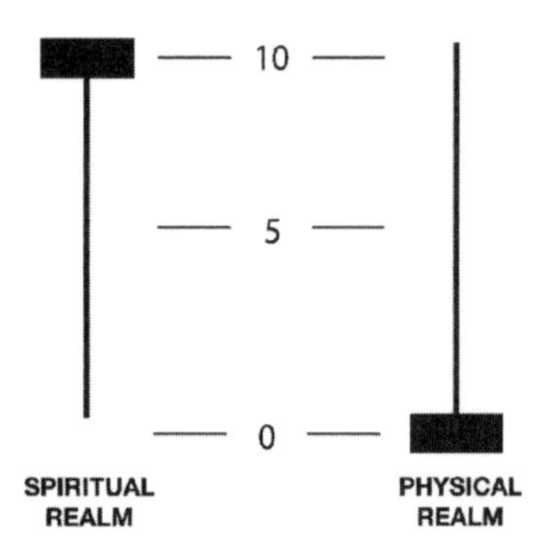

Then there are some who live a permanent life of confusion and being misunderstood or misdiagnosed—these are usually the people our society labels mentally ill. Others enter this state every so often when having deep experiences of the Spirit.

I wonder if it is possible to experience life with our settings set to this:

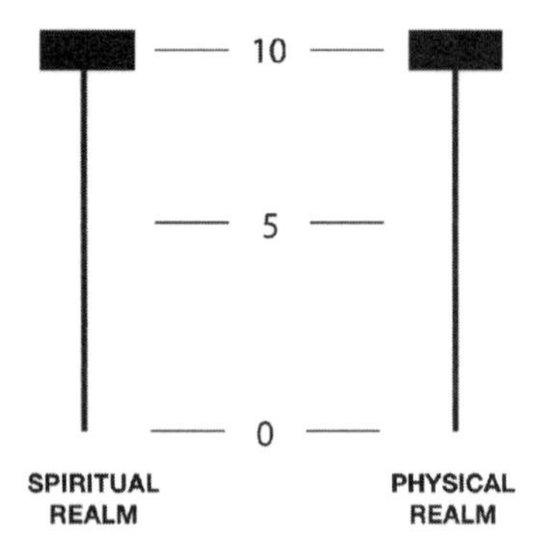

I wonder if we can be simultaneously aware of all the realms where God is operating. I wonder if this is really what practicing the Presence of God is all about. I wonder if this is what it means to experience heaven on earth.

What if we learned to turn up our dimmer switch on the spiritual realm while still living grounded in reality: the reality of living in one world, not two? Heaven on earth—not us down here and heaven up there somewhere. What if we could get our dimmer switch of the unseen to go up a notch? Can we get it from a 1 to a 2 or a 6 to a 7?

Yes. But to do so, we've got to train our spiritual awareness.

THE GYM OF THE SPIRIT

I've never met anyone who sees all the time with full accuracy at a 10, nor have I ever met anyone who exists at 0. Even non-believers have some awareness of the unseen. The atheist rational empiricist can be aware of the mystical realm but might call it unexplained or yet-to-be explained. People who operate at a 2 and people who operate at a 6 might see the same thing differently; when they compare notes, they might assume they each saw something different. The difference is the level of maturity or operation of the gift. And the goal is to train and grow the gift.

> For though by this time you ought to be teachers, you have need again for someone

> to teach you the elementary principles of the oracles of God, and you have come to need milk and not solid food. For everyone who partakes [only] of milk is not accustomed to the word of righteousness, for he is an infant. But solid food is for the mature, who because of practice have their senses trained to discern good and evil (Hebrews 5:12-14, NASB).

To handle the solid food, we need to train our senses and our discernment. The Greek word for "trained" here is *gymnazō* from which we get the word "gymnasium." Basically, we need to take our discernment to the gym.

As with physical training, our exercises should be varied and intense if we are to shock our discernment muscle into growth. We also need to increase our flexibility so that we can take on more intensity and grow stronger.

None of this is comfortable.

We have to be careful of a few things as well. Repeating the same exercise with the same weights for the same number of reps may stunt us. Another way to stunt ourselves is by comparison. You know those attention seeking gym addicts? The ones who grunt loudly and clank their weights down and pose in front of the mirrors? They are intimidating, and it's silly to compare ourselves to them. I like that Planet Fitness gyms are anti-lunk zones; everyone is encouraged to get healthy, from the newbie to the veteran weightlifter. The Church should foster a similar, safe environment to build our strength. We do not need a competition track for our Holy Spirit athletes, and neither do we need to diminish others to make our gifting seem better.

The goal of faith is to grow *with* each other and to encourage each other as we train together. That includes admitting when we get it wrong—when we injure ourselves or others. Anyone who is "always right" in their discernment or seeing is a really scary person, not because of their ability but because of the absence of humility. We must be willing to be corrected. We don't want to build muscles the wrong way; that can lead to injury—in the physical and in the spiritual.

THE MYSTICAL IN SCRIPTURE

The Bible is full of mystic realities. Let's look at a few:

Genesis 3:1 We gloss over the shock in the garden when a serpent speaks to Eve. We rightly get caught up in the real message of the story, but seriously! What would you do if a snake spoke to you today?

Genesis 6:4 This verse mentions the Nephilim: the giants. We can speculate about who the Nephilim were (some believe they were the fallen angels), but my point in mentioning them is that they aren't exactly part of our contemporary, everyday visible realm. But they are in Scripture.

Numbers 22:28 God opens the mouth of Balaam's donkey, and the donkey speaks. We could say that it is actually God speaking, but regardless of whether God activated a dormant function of the beast or temporarily allowed the beast to speak, the reality is: the donkey speaks. The donkey asks Balaam a question. The donkey argues with him. And the donkey wins the argument. This is not a scene from *Shrek* the movie, this is the inerrant Word of God. The most shocking piece though? It's that Balaam isn't shocked that his donkey is speaking!

2 Kings 2:23-24 Forty-two boys tease Elisha for being bald. He curses them, and two bears come out of the woods and kill the children. What? We can explain this as the misused power of a prophet operating in an old covenant. But how do our hermeneutics explain how nature responds to the curse of a prophet "in the name of the Lord?"

And there are plenty of New Testament examples as well:

Matthew 2:1-2 The Magi find the Messiah by following a star, and then hear from God in a dream to not tell Herod where He is.

Matthew 17:27 Jesus pays His taxes by finding money in a fish.

Matthew 27:51 The moment Jesus dies, the veil of the Holy of Holies is torn in two. We know that this represents the shattering of the old covenant, but there is another important element here; the veil was torn from top to bottom—from Heaven to earth.

Matthew 27:52-53 Right after the veil is torn, the dead rise up from their graves and walk around.

Certifiably weird, all of it. Yet we can get so familiar with these stories that we almost become blasé about deep mysteries. The mystical references in the Bible are full of invitational mystery. If we're willing, we can go deeper into them and better understand God's heart.

CLOSE ENCOUNTERS

Mystical things can point us toward our mystical God. As we encounter His goodness, the unseen becomes seen—and visible to those who are looking for God. The reason for signs and wonders and miracles is to point people to someone, to lead people into an encounter with God—not just park around the seemingly weird stuff He does.

The world is hungry for a revelation of the mystical realm, but they often end up with the dark version of it because the Church has been so afraid of all things mystical. We need to share the light. If it is not visible to our natural eyes, we have to learn to see it. We can't let fear keep us from accepting God's invitation to explore His mysteries with Him.

The open secret is that Jesus is at the center of all we believe; He is the plumb line of our experience. In all of our mystical realm experiences, we must keep the main thing the main thing: Jesus is King, and His Kingdom is advancing.

Years ago, when I was a cop on the streets of Belfast, I was waiting to exit the police station. I won't go into all the details, but at the time, we had to be careful when we left the station gates. As the gates opened, I stepped outside. Immediately, I encountered what *appeared* to be a nun. She quietly spoke to me and told me not to go outside. I stepped back into the station and told my partner what just happened.

He looked out to the road. The nun had disappeared. I also looked up and down the road, but the nun was nowhere to be seen. The hairs were sticking up on both of our necks, so we closed the gates and called for backup. Moments later, the backup arrived and discovered a discarded command-wire IED on the route that we were to take. I believe we either encountered the fastest nun that ever existed, or we encountered an angel who had taken human form.

Many people tell stories of this sort of encounter. "Someone" showed up and saved them from disaster. I believe that the unseen world is just as real as the seen world. I believe that it can encounter us and we can encounter it, and I believe that all of this points to encountering God.

As believers in the inerrant Word of God, we should all believe in a mystical reality. There are things we simply cannot rationalize. Bill Johnson of Bethel Church in Redding, California, says that we can have understanding or we can have peace—but we seldom get both because His peace surpasses understanding.

We just don't have to understand everything. We are a supernatural people. We believe in a God we have not seen. Yet we try to convince others intellectually and rationally to believe in this God. People don't need a rational argument; they need an encounter with the unseen God who is made manifest through works that *can* be seen and experienced. When that happens, the unseen is made seen.

Think of those dimmer switches; we must keep growing, training, and increasing our "settings" to better see and share the light of the Kingdom.

2: THE IMAGINATION

One of the greatest golfers on the planet is Tiger Woods. His father was a lieutenant colonel in the army, and if it weren't for someone inventing the game of golf, Tiger may have followed in his father's footsteps and joined the military. However, someone *did* invent golf. Someone imagined a game, others added to that imagination, and the game of golf was born. Tiger Woods is arguably the best player in a game that was once only played in the unseen realm of someone's imagination. Were it not for that imagination, Tiger may have not even known he is great at something.

What if the things we create in our imagination will be manifest in generations to come? What if the things we imagine become part of people's callings and destinities?

A REDEEMED IMAGINATION

The word "image" is at the heart of the word "imagination." To imagine a thing is to picture it. Imagination is a real, valid way of seeing—and it is powerful.

To work well with our imagination, we have to break off the lie from the devil that says it is impure. In fact, if you have believed that, take a moment and break that lie off of yourself. Invite the Holy Spirit to redeem your imagination.

You're going to want a redeemed imagination because this thing is *powerful*. What we imagine creates reality. We need to start believing and behaving like this is true and using our imagination for good. What if you started imagining what it would be like to fully live in your calling? What if you imagine what it's like when you meet the person of your dreams? What if you imagine your city fully devoted to God?

Pick something good you want to imagine: maybe it's something about your calling, your spouse, or your city. Maybe it's something else. Picture a future and a hope for that outcome. Now, start behaving toward it and speaking toward it.

Not only does your imagination create reality, but your words do as well. You've heard the saying: our words create worlds. The power of an anointed, inspired word is enough to say, "Let there be light"...and for light to appear.

Proverbs 18:21 tells us that death and life are in the power of the tongue. Make no mistake about it: you can kill with the tongue. You can also give new life and hope with it, too. We must understand how powerful it is if we speak negative things over our own lives.

Whenever you are tempted to speak a negative word over your life, flip it to a positive. Instead of saying "I am stupid" try "I am smart." Instead of saying "I'm hopeless," try "I am full of hope." If the full positive opposite seems too much, ease into it with statements like, "I am continually learning new things" and "I am choosing hope."

As you become more accustomed to speaking the positive in your life, expand it. Get specific. I say of myself "I've been put on this earth to give people courage to do what's in their hearts. I'm a revivalist. I am here to see the revival of God in the Church, on the streets, and in every marketplace in the world."

This kind of imagination requires changing how we think. We have to give ourselves permission to imagine—to dream while we're awake.

THE POWER OF OUR IMAGINATION

The song "Just My Imagination" is a great song but a lousy way of thinking about this tool. Our redeemed and sanctified imaginations have the power to create on earth what we see in the heavenly realm.

Unredeemed imaginations are downright dangerous. You have heard that it was, "YOU SHALL NOT COMMIT ADULTERY". But Jesus warns us:

> but I say to you that everyone who looks at a woman with lust for her has already committed adultery with her in his heart" (Matthew 5:27-28 NASB).

This verse tells us a lot of things. One: there is no room for self-righteousness. Those who might say, "Well, I have never actually slept with another woman" don't get to feel holier than the person physically caught in adultery. Two: when you do something in your imagination, it is as real as if you did it in the seen world.

Our imagination has the power to create reality.

In Hebrews 11:1 KJV we are told that "faith is the substance of things hoped for, the evidence of things not seen." The word *substance* is the Greek word *hypostasis*. It is sometimes translated as *assurance* or *nature*, but what exactly is it? What is faith?

Faith is often considered a blind, irrational leap in the dark—devoid of intellectual content. But faith is a real thing of substance that exists in an unseen realm and can be manifest in a seen realm. That is the context of *hypostasis* is Hebrews 1:3 where Jesus is described as the very substance of God. Jesus manifested in the seen realm what we had not—until He came—been able to see apart from in the mystical realm: God. Jesus was not only the substance of God in mystical terms, but He was made flesh for everyone to see.

Here are several ways to say the same thing:

- Faith is a substantial thing that exists in the unseen realm.
- Faith is the substance of things not seen.
- The unseen realm is as real as the seen realm.

This unseen is real. And it is powerful.

BEYOND THE MATERIAL

In addition to breaking off the lie that the imagination is an evil thing, we must also challenge any materialist tendencies we might have. Materialism tells us that we have to be able to experience something with our natural senses for it to be real. If that's true, then we'd have to write off most of Scripture—and most of our mystical experiences.

Have you heard healing testimonies of people "reaching" into Heaven, grabbing a body part they need, and bringing it to earth? What if that's not just a prophetic act? What if you can actually reach into that realm and grab the heart, lung, liver, kidneys, or eyes that you need? What if you are deaf and you enter that mystical realm, pick out the ears you need, put them on your body, and return to earth totally healed and able to hear?

And what if you could access that realm for other people?

If we are materialists and believe that something can only exist in this material, visible world, we will limit ourselves to only this material, visible world. We have to break the materialist mindset and see that our prayers and thoughts also have substance. In fact, neuroscientists like Dr. Caroline Leaf have proven that our thoughts actually create physical matter.

God has known this all along, of course; He set it all up. God had an idea, and He spoke the world into being. If we think from heaven to earth, our "immaterial" thoughts are actually creating material things, and the idea that we can pull "things" from heaven starts to sound much more possible, probable even.

We all know this prayer:

> "Our Father in Heaven, hallowed be Your name, Your kingdom come, Your will be done, on earth as it is in Heaven" (Matthew 6:9-10 NIV).

What if that isn't a rote prayer but an invitation? What if that invitation to access Heaven is so that we can give the goods to others?

However, we can't give away what we don't have. You've heard Peter's famous line to the lame beggar: "'Silver or gold I do not have, but what I do have I give you.'" (Acts 3:6 NIV). Peter knew he had access to heaven where the man's healing was. He knew he could "cash the check."

What about us? We'll pray for that friend with cancer. We'll pray for that couple's marriage, but do we actually have the "cash" in our spirit accounts? Have we been making deposits of faith? Have we been making heavenly transfers?

I'd like to suggest that we don't have the solutions because we haven't learned how to access heaven. To do so, we must renew our minds and hearts and imaginations. And we must remember how good God is and how much He wants to show us and share with us.

OPEN THEISM

This is the gist of open theism: God loves us. He loves us so much that He gave us free will to love Him back and to make our own choices. Because of that, He made His plans for our future conditional upon our choices and actions. Yes, God knows everything, but He can choose to *not* know what we will do as we make our own choices.

People protest that if God is omniscient, He must know our choices. What if He is so all-knowing that he can choose what *not* to know? If He can choose to forget our sins, could He also choose to let us make our choices without predetermining them? If we believe in a God who gives us life for death, the paradox of His knowing and unknowing shouldn't be too much of an issue.

Yet for much of Church history, we have seen our life trajectory as a single railway line. If all goes well, we chug along in the right direction. But if we blow it and derail, we think we've wrecked the will of God for our lives. We think we blew it because we didn't marry that person or because we divorced that person or because we once had a marijuana brownie. In addition to the shame we feel for our actions, we think God has given up on us and there's no getting back on that single track.

When we think this way, we are misinterpreting Jeremiah 29:11:

> "For I know the plans I have for you," declares the LORD, "plans to prosper you and not to harm you, plans to give you hope and a future. (NIV)"

That Scripture does *not* say that God has *a* plan for your life. It says "I know the *plans* I have for you." Plans: plural. More than one. Guess what? God has a great imagination—He invented it! Even if we think we've messed up, He has all sorts of other great ideas to give us hope and a future.

But we tend to camp where we derailed and crashed. We pitch our tent by the wreckage and think our future is over. God is like "Oh! Don't you know how many marvelous plans I have for you? Don't you know the dreams I have for you?"

I want to suggest that there isn't just one railroad track of life choices that will get you to your destination—your destiny. I want to suggest that from this exact moment forward, every possible outcome exists to prosper your life; there is a realm filled with possibilities for your good future.

But we don't see this realm if we remain stuck in determinist and predetermined thinking. If you are a parent, have you tried predetermining your children's life? Good luck with that. It's not the heart of a good father or mother to predetermine all outcomes for their children. Everyone must learn to make their own healthy choices, even if that means they sometimes make unhealthy ones.

And whether or not you have children, you can ask yourself, "Where am I living from a determinist mindset?" Have you locked yourself into any past decisions? Have you confused your identity with your behavior?

Question: where does the past exist? Answer: only in your mind. Your past only exists in your mind. But if you continually bring your past into your present, you are going to affect your future. If you want to let your past go, you might have to do some work. You might need to forgive a zillion people. You might need counseling or SOZO inner healing. We must renew our minds to see that our past failures do not limit our futures.

Yet many of us have become addicted to our precious hurts. Remember cave-dwelling Gollum from *Lord of the Rings*?

We act like him with our past failures. In a cooing tone, we say, "Oh, remember that failure? My precious! I keep saying I want someone to take it away, but I really don't want them to because then I'd have to change." Then the cooing tone changes to a snarl, "And I don't want to change or be vulnerable or trust anyone!" And back to an ingratiating coo, "So I'm just going to keep my precious past failure with me. Oh, my precious!"

Yikes.

If we let go of our past—our victim mindset and our failures—we are free to imagine and take hold of the good plans God has for us.

Open theism is such a beautiful glimpse into divine imagination. God is so big. He "is able to do immeasurably more than all we ask or imagine" (Ephesians 3:20 NIV). And He invites us to partner with Him to imagine that "immeasurably more"—even if we derail.

As we grow our redeemed, powerful, heaven-aligned imagination, we will begin to see the scope of Kingdom reality.

3: DISCERNING THE *REAL* REALITY

Many children see images or monsters or "invisible" friends, and often those children are taught out of such sight by well-meaning parents and caregivers who are afraid of the mystical realm.

Fear is one of the main enemies of seeing in the spirit. We are afraid that the devil and darkness have the upper hand.

NEGATIVITY BIAS

If we encounter two things of relatively equal importance—one negative and one positive—we'll focus more on the negative than the positive. That is negativity bias. Some of it is natural instinct, or a flight-or-flight need to be able to quickly assess a threat. Some of it becomes habitual through practice.

This bias occurs in our spiritual perception too. Many of us are more aware of the darkness than the light. We walk through life acutely aware of what is wrong with others. We sense the "bad" atmospheres of streets, neighborhoods, and towns. If we are perpetually engaging darkness, is it possible that we are letting darkness determine how we experience the spiritual realm? We should be focused on bringing heaven to earth, not looking for hell on earth.

Sometimes, an increased understanding of darkness is necessary. My friend pastors a church in California, and they are inundated with witchcraft. They have covens praying against them. Witches come to their services, leaving amulets and cursing the building. The church is right in the middle of darkness, and they need to be extra attuned to what the enemy's doing along with what God is doing—but they always pay more attention to God.

Even if you are operating in thick darkness like that, if you're only ever aware of the darkness, then you might want to make some adjustments in your spiritual sight. Darkness is the absence of light, and even if you are moving in a place of darkness, you are bringing light, so you want to keep your eyes on the light and stay in the light and bring that light into the darkness. You want to continually be asking God, "What are You doing here? What is heaven up to?"

THE DANIEL RATIO

There is and has been plenty of darkness in this world. King Nebuchadnezzar of Babylon is a prime example. He worshiped demonic gods and set up shrines to himself. Not the most noble of leaders. Yet Daniel positioned himself to serve this king—to share heaven with him. Despite being surrounded by a kingdom that celebrated evil, Daniel walked in the light, untouched. Today you have believers complaining about working for a boss who isn't a Christian!

We forget that our light is not extinguished in darkness. Within recent memory, Christians have been afraid to go into a bar where they might encounter sinners and get "slimed." I am so glad we're mostly over that kind of thinking, but we still have a ways to go.

Daniel served a demonic king amidst more evil than most of us can imagine, but he served faithfully and without fear of the evil rubbing off on him. He kept his integrity, he kept His eyes and ears on God, and he was able to share divine wisdom. He established a reputation as a wise man.

When Nebuchadnezzar got fed up with the opinions of his magicians who could not accurately interpret his dreams, he asked for Daniel's sight and insight. The king valued intellect, and Daniel was smart. He was also smarter—and wiser—than the magicians around him. In fact, Nebuchadnezzar found Daniel ten times wiser than the magicians in his kingdom.

I call that the Daniel ratio: being ten times wiser in the spirit than anyone operating from darkness. I think that Christians should be pursuing a Daniel ratio. We should cultivate natural intellect *and* supernatural wisdom.

Across Church history, we see a trend: revival happens, but a generation into it, people get fed up with the signs, wonders, miracles, and interpretations and they say we need to be more intellectual. Then the next generation gets fed up with the non-supernatural intellectualism and says we need revival. What would happen if we cultivated both?

Like Nebuchadnezzar, our culture is fed up with powerless opinions. Kings and queens and presidents and prime ministers are desperately longing for the people of God to stand up and not just share their opinions about their dreams but to truly interpret, unpack, and show how to apply those interpretations to their current reality. The world is crying out for people who don't just opine, but who can use the supernatural power to tell them their dreams.

Meanwhile, the Church is running scared, worried about entertaining the devil. My Bible says, "greater is He who is in you than he who is in the world (I John 4:6 NASB). I'm pretty sure yours does too.

We have nothing to fear. As long as we keep Christ the center, we are safe and secure in the *real* reality of heaven.

DISCERNMENT

We need to grow in the gift of discernment with grace and mercy. As we learn, we will mess up. That's just part of learning. So, we have to check our egos at the door. If I enter the gym filled with my ego, I will try to lift weights that people 20 years younger than me are lifting. I might be successful—for a moment—but if I'm lifting my ego too, I will certainly get hurt and I'll probably end up blaming someone else for my decision.

Let's be teachable; it will save us a lot of wasted time and, more importantly, a potentially wasted destiny.

Discernment has played a big part of my life, but I've screwed it up so much it's laughable. I am not writing about it as an expert; I'm writing as someone who is hoping you don't have to fight the battles that I've fought. If I can save you some agony, wonderful.

Discernment, prophecy, and words of knowledge are all revelatory gifts. We operate these gifts in our individual ways, and often, the way we operate one is similar to the way we operate the others. Some people see images in their mind's eye, some people hear things in their hearts, some people feel sensations, and some people just know stuff. If you normally prophesy by seeing pictures or images, you might say, "I am seeing a picture of The Wizard of Oz, the man behind the curtain...." And if that's how you move in prophecy then discernment will likely come to you that way as well.

Unless it doesn't.

I know—not really helpful but stay with me. Some people recognize that they've received a prophetic word because they almost always receive revelation visually; they prophesy using a picture. But these "visual" people can receive a word of discernment differently, and they recognize it as discernment because they feel/hear/sense something. They might not know what it means, but they know it is something.

So, you might experience all of the gifts in a similar way or you might experience them in different ways. You don't have to figure out some "correct" way to operate them, but you do have to become familiar with how the gifts work through you individually.

I want to emphasize: learning how to use our gifts is different from the idea that we learn the gifts—we don't. They are gifts, and like all the gifts of the Spirit, discernment is not a result of nurture or effort or upbringing. That's called "reading people." In my experience, if someone does not know the difference between discernment and reading people, they can do a fair bit of harm. Allow me to tell you a story to illustrate what it is to read people.

READING PEOPLE

Sam was an alcoholic. He worked a job with no destiny or purpose. No future. No hope. What little pay he received, Sam spent on unholy things, trying to numb the disappointments of his life.

Like many men who worked hard 40 hours a week, Sam spent Friday evenings at the local pub, magically transforming his paycheck into amber nectar. He always hoped that this would be the week when those six little lottery numbers he chose would metamorphose from his children's birth dates into millions of dollars.

Every night Sam came home, his children would try to guess how much amber nectar their father had drunk. One glass was certainly not enough; one bottle would mean certain sleep. It was the amount in between where the great unknown lay. Eight drinks might mean laughter. Twelve might mean a release of uncontrollable rage. The children never knew, and they could certainly never ask. The question, "How many whiskeys did you have tonight, Dad?" could lead to a brisk hand across the cheek, or it could mean watching their father, their hero, cry in shame and weakness. So they just had to **know**. *It was an unspoken requirement of the family. If one of the children didn't know, he or she was seen as uncaring, inconsiderate, and heartless.*

If you had an alcoholic father or an abusive authority figure in your life, that story is all too familiar. You've figured out how to walk through life reading anyone who could potentially hurt you. You've built up a defense system that kicks into high gear any time that past wound gets jabbed.

There is a big difference between operating from the fruit of brokenness and the gift of discernment.

I would argue that much of what the Church has accepted as discernment is in fact reading people. Reading people is a coping skill designed to help you get through life. Discernment is *not* a coping skill; it is a gift from God to advance the Kingdom and help bring heaven to earth. A Spirit-filled believer, operating in what they think is discernment, will often say things like, "I just feel there's something off. I don't know what it is about that person, but I'm feeling there's something off. Hmm...Jezebel. I think it's the spirit of Jezebel." And they pass that off as discernment.

No! The "I'm just not sure about this person" kind of line is really someone saying that they feel the same thing they felt in their past, and they do not want to get hurt again. That's reading people. That's not the gift of discernment.

The only way to let go of your past hurt is to forgive the one(s) who hurt you. If you don't want bad past experiences to keep distorting your present and your future, it is 100% necessary to forgive those who have hurt you. Even if you still can't trust that person. Even if they are no longer alive. Even if they don't deserve it. Bitterness and unforgiveness will stunt your spiritual growth and turn into judgment, which we'll talk more about a bit later.

FOCUS ON HEAVEN, NOT HELL

Many years ago, when my wife and I got baptized in the Holy Spirit, we began to learn the stuff of the Spirit. Rachel and I are both pretty discerning people, though we didn't know how to use that gift. We would strain at gnats to try and get the proper "discernment" on people, churches, meetings, or whatever. We would say things like, "I noticed there was a slight inflection on their voice, did you hear that? I think that revealed their heart for…" And we were accurate, but it was only dark stuff—the veneer of discernment. We were only capable of pointing out the dark spots.

The problem is that is exactly the job description of Satan, to make us point at darkness and say, "I'd like you all to focus on this dark spot right here." He is an accuser who focuses on sin, failings, and accusation, and we didn't know that we were partnering with him. The devil doesn't want you to look at the good, he wants you to obsess about the bad.

It took us quite a while to press through the darkness, to identify and focus on the good parts, and to pull them to the surface and declare a future and a hope. That is more in line with the person of the Holy Spirit, the Giver of this gift of discernment.

The gift of discernment is about seeing what heaven is doing. It doesn't take the gift of discernment to see what the devil is doing. Otherwise, the devil would have the gift of discernment. The devil and his minions all know what he is about: "The thief comes only to steal and kill and destroy." (John 10:10 NASB). Actually, the word for "kill" is better translated as "slaughter." The devil is not just content with killing; he's out to slaughter us. In vivid contrast, Jesus says in the second half of that verse, "I came that they may have life, and have [it] abundantly."

Discernment is always searching for what heaven is doing, not for what the devil is doing.

All of us can use every spiritual gift; if you are born again and born of the Spirit, then He lives inside you. He didn't arrive in you without one or two of the gifts, saying *I'll just leave those for somebody else*. The Holy Spirit fully indwells you, as does all of His power and gifts. And when the Holy Spirit is within you, He can show up and manifest in whatever gift He wants.

If you'd like to learn more about this, I highly recommend Francis Frangipane's book *The Three Battlegrounds*. When I first read it, I was offended, which I've learned is actually a good sign. I was offended because Frangipane was challenging me on stuff that I wasn't sure I should be challenged on. I mean, when "discerning" people discern, they *know*! Right? Not necessarily.

The Greek word *diákrisis*, translated as discernment, means "to decide after judging." This can get tricky because the gift of discernment is not about passing judgment in the sense of determining whether or not something is wrong. It's about judging whether something is aligned with heaven. We will discern negative things, but we do not pass judgment on them.

This might sound contradictory, but you will never grow in your gift of discernment if you do not eradicate, abhor, and reject judgment. Of course, none of us think we are judgmental, we all just think we know something that another is blind to.

To trust us with the secrets of people's hearts, our loving Father needs us to be trustworthy.

HONOR VS. JUDGMENT

This is where the culture of honor comes in. I tell you my truth—not what I think or discern or judge to be your truth. If you want to destroy relationships, keep telling people what you think they are like, what they truly mean, and why they behave like they do. It will shatter trust and halt revelation. Intimacy is created through the sharing of truth, not assumptions.

Can you be trusted with other people's secrets—without judging them? Without saying or thinking the equivalent of, "Hey, your thoughts or actions make you a bad person, and I am self-righteously amazing." Because judgment really is about self-righteousness. To judge is to consider someone less than ourselves. If we can move away from judgment, then we can start to grow in discernment. Fair warning: it's hard. It's hard because as you grow and as your switch of discernment goes up, you then start to see little secrets and hidden things, and you have to re-learn all over again not to judge. And that's just the baseline. We are not only *not* to judge others; we are to honor them.

In places where Jesus could only do a few miracles, the implication is that there was no honor; people perceived Him from His past, not from His heavenly identity. Honor is the bedrock for starting and growing in the gift of discernment. Honor is about being humble and putting someone else above you—not assessing their motives and actions.

We give honor in humility not from a place of low self-esteem, but from a place of wanting to understand others.

My wife and I have met some "famous," prophetic, discerning people. Everyone we know does the same thing when they are about to meet these people; they spend the time beforehand confessing all their sins, deeply worshipping, praying in tongues, and trying to spiritually cleanse themselves so that when they walk into the room where the famous person of discernment is, they will not point at them and shout "LUST!" or whatever. The more we get to know some of these prophetic, discerning people, however, the more we realize that's not how they operate.

One couple we know are probably the most prophetic people we have ever met. They are amazing Kingdom people, but they prefer to remain anonymous. They came to stay with us in 2005, and we'd never had a conversation before then. At first, they just sat in our living room in silence.

I'm thinking, "I hope they don't see inside of me. What are they going to see about my children? Is there an atmosphere in the room?"

We started talking and getting to know them. The woman is incredibly discerning, and I thought this was a great opportunity to learn, so I asked her, "What do you do when you meet someone and you get some insight into their day, their month, their year, their life?"

She replied, "Do you have permission to do that?"

I said, "Well, if it just comes to me, I imagine I'm OK..."

And in the gentlest way possible she told me, "No, no, no dear. You need to ask the Father if you have permission to see those things."

From that point on, I started to ask the Father if I had permission to see things in people's lives. My mistake had been to assume that because this was a gift of the Holy Spirit, I had permission to see and make a judgment. I have learned that these first "knowings" are not really the gift; they are the access point for the gift—the doorway into something greater. What you do in this doorway when you meet someone is momentous and will determine whether you can access the inner sanctum of knowing. It is like you need to enter an access code, and the access code is to not look at the veneer but to press through to see the heart of the Father. Will you judge or will you honor? If I meet someone and feel all their hurts and all their pain, I do not get to judge them. I say, "Father, do I have permission to see this? I want to know what You are saying about what I see and sense. I want to know what heaven is doing." Getting over judgment is vital.

Also vital is realizing that that the first thing that you will discern—whether in a dance club on Saturday night or in a church service on Sunday morning—wherever you go, the first thing you're going to discern is *yourself*. The first thing you're going to discern is yourself and your reaction to whatever is happening.

No matter how many times I tell people this, they always think that they are different, that their discernment is actually some higher grade than everyone else's. Since I can't scream it from the rooftops in this book, I'll put in in all caps: THE FIRST THING YOU WILL DISCERN IS YOURSELF AND *YOUR* REACTION TO WHATEVER HUMAN OR SPIRITUAL STIMULI IS HAPPENING!

A couple of years ago, I attended a pastors' and leaders' event. Let's just say I didn't enjoy it. When I walked into the sanctuary, it was like walking into a room packed with 700 Chihuahuas all yapping, yapping, yapping at the conference leaders, trying to get noticed. At one point, I was asked to come to the stage with 10 other people, and by the end of that day, six people had come up to me and handed me their books, hoping that I would give them to the leader of the conference. I couldn't stand the pack of Chihuahuas trying to get recognized.

Of course, I was forgetting that I was the chief Chihuahua, right? I forgot that I wasn't discerning everybody else's stuff; I was discerning *my* stuff—my own insecurity and seeking after recognition.

It can be tough to remember and admit every single time: the first thing we discern is ourselves. But once we recognize that we are discerning our response to our environment—to whatever spiritual and emotional stimuli is happening—then we can move past it. Then we will become aware of what the enemy is doing.

Now, you don't need discernment to know what the enemy is doing; I have relatives who don't know Jesus and they are very, very, very good at picking up what the enemy is doing. In fact, I would say my entire culture in Ireland is very good at picking up what the enemy is doing. So again, we need to understand once we've discerned ourselves, the next thing we discern is the enemy's intent to steal, kill (slaughter), and destroy.

Then we can push past all that and see what heaven is doing. What heaven is doing is *the* most important thing. Tactically, as warriors, the most important thing to understand is not what the enemy's plans are, but what the General's plans are: what Jesus' plans are. If we can align ourselves with those plans, it makes life and the fight far easier. I'm not saying we need to completely ignore what the enemy is doing, but I *am* saying we have to push past that as we grow in discernment to see what Heaven is doing. A sign of growth in discernment is that you are talking more about what God is up to than what the enemy is up to.

So, if we let go of judgment, and if we remember that we will first discern our own reaction to spiritual stimuli, *then* we actually move forward. Then we can grow and get to a deeper place with discernment. People who call themselves discerning but have not learned this aren't very fun to be around, unless you want to know what's wrong with everybody. People operating in healthy discernment are the happiest people around; they are looking into the spiritual realm and can see what God is doing and how He is at work—even in broken lives and circumstances. The time for Puddleglum discerners is over.

I can't emphasize this enough: on the journey of growing in discernment, the first thing you will discern is yourself. Then you'll discern the darkness—the activity of hell. *Then* you'll begin to recognize heaven—the light in the darkness. It takes a bit of practice to straight up discern what heaven is doing.

Growing in discernment will require each of us to learn how to keep asking the questions about what God is doing, not simply what we feel or we see the devil doing.

YOUR GYM MEMBERSHIP

Discernment is the genesis of the "seer" ability. Or to say it another way: being a seer is an extension of the gift of discernment. So, if you want to see, you have to grow in discernment. And to grow those muscles, you have to take them to the *gymnazō*. You have to just keep practicing and doing the reps.

Earlier, I mentioned that we have to forgive those who hurt us. We need to stop coping with our past and actually conquer it. We have to heal if we want to grow in a healthy direction and not hobble around with our atrophied injuries of the spirit.

This is similar to the physical: if we injure our elbow and try to do even a low-weight bench press, we are just going to compound the injury. In fact, we might do damage that seriously affects our future growth.

We must stop living as small people locked in the restrictions of our own unforgiveness. Paul said it well:

> Dear, dear Corinthians, I can't tell you how much I long for you to enter this wide-open, spacious life. We didn't fence you in. The smallness you feel comes from within you. Your lives aren't small, but you're living them in a small way. I'm speaking as plainly as I can and with great affection. Open up your lives. Live openly and expansively! (2 Corinthians 6:11-13 MSG).

We must press through our hurts and betrayals to see what the Father is doing, not what the devil is doing. Once we do this, I believe the unseen can open up for us.

One of the biggest mistakes people make with the spiritual gifts is thinking they come to us fully formed, just add water. Remember Hebrews 5:14 and *gymnazō?* We must train our senses. We must use our "gym membership" to train our discernment. And as we do, we have to accept that we're not going to be insta-athletes. It's going to take some practice and lots of reps to build the muscle of healthy discernment.

Someone I knew once received a picture they felt was from the Lord. They interpreted it to mean a complete change for their whole family. When they told me this, they expected me to bless the revelation and their interpretation. They were not prepared for me to challenge the interpretation, which would have removed their entire family from healthy relationships. I did not feel that such a move was the heart of the Father for them.

Seeing is about more than just what we see—the revelation. It's also about the interpretation and the application of that revelation. And guess what? We might get one or more parts of that process wrong. That can be hard for us to admit, but it is especially hard with the gift of discernment. Knowing that we might get it wrong requires humility and a teachable spirit.

If we want to discern the *real* reality, we've got to keep using our gym membership to train our senses, get past ourselves, focus on heaven, and walk in honor as we bring light into dark places.

4: MACRO-TO-MICRO THINKING

I teach our leaders to think and believe from macro to micro. This is especially important when it comes to discernment. In fact, I'd like to suggest that what you believe about Jesus, the Father, the Holy Spirit, and the Cross will affect how you operate in the gift of discernment.

Do you believe the Cross was totally sufficient? Do you believe God still needs to punish? Do you believe that the coming of Pentecost in the book of Acts was good...but maybe not enough? Your answers to those questions (your macro beliefs) will shape how you actually minister in your gift of discernment (micro).

For example: victorious eschatology. That's a fancy way of saying that we're not waiting around for any more punishment in the end times. Many of us believe that the punishment God poured out on earth happened in 70 AD, and we're not waiting for any more of it.[1] More of my macro beliefs: the Cross was completely sufficient; the Kingdom arrived with Jesus, and it has been growing for 2,000 years; I'm not waiting for the return of Jesus to usher in a future Kingdom; I am waiting and longing for Jesus to return for a Church that has manifested His Kingdom, where earth is like heaven.

Do I believe He's returning? Oh yes, I absolutely believe He's coming back, but I'm not waiting for Jesus to come back to fight a battle in geographic Israel to defeat the enemy when the Cross was completely sufficient to defeat the enemy in the first place. I am waiting on Jesus coming back to receive His final reward and to see all of His enemies placed under His feet. I believe that the Cross was a victory, and we are here to continue the works of Jesus and to destroy the works of the defeated devil. Those macro beliefs affect my micro thoughts and actions: the choices I make, how I minister, how I discern—everything.

YOU ARE UNPUNISHABLE

I teach and practice and am growing in a culture of honor. One pillar of a culture of honor is that you are absolutely unpunishable. 100% unpunishable. God's not looking for justice

1 If you'd like to learn more, check out the book *Victorious Eschatology* by Harold R. Eberle & Martin Trench.

when you sin; otherwise, His forgiveness isn't enough. And we certainly don't have to add our penance to His forgiveness.

But if I have a macro belief that God is really angry at the entire universe—that He's really mad and can't wait to punish humanity—then I minister with the discernment of judgment, the very thing that prevents us from moving deeper into the seer realm.

My macro belief in the new covenant means that the laws under the old covenant are no longer applicable. We now have one law: Love. We are to love God, our neighbor, and ourselves. For example, I don't tithe to escape judgment (I'm going to use the word "tithe," but please don't get caught up in an exact ten percent). I don't tithe to escape judgment; I tithe to access blessings. The enemy comes to steal, kill, and destroy, but Jesus said He came that we would have life and have it abundantly. So, if I want an abundant life, it's probably a good idea to be a good steward of what I've been given. My macro beliefs about tithing begin with my relationship with an abundant Father.

Macro thinking about punishment can play out in many ways. Take marriage. I only sleep with my wife; I do not sleep with other women. I don't make this choice because I might get caught and punished; I make this choice because I want my marriage to be amazing. I don't spend time with my wife because I don't want her to nag me. I spend time with her because I want our marriage to be connected, intimate, and wonderful.

All of our micro thinking begins with our macro thinking. If your macro-level beliefs about God are of a mad, vindictive being ready to bring judgment on the Earth, your micro-level actions and ministering will reflect that.

When I think about things that are to come, I align my thoughts with the declaration of the coming of Jesus: "Of the increase of His government and of peace there shall be no end" (Isaiah 9:7a KJV). If your discernment doesn't bring an increase of His government and of peace, back away. Back away until you can get to that place.

YOU ARE NOT A WORM

I live just outside of Chicago. It is the most beautiful city I have ever seen, and the people are magnificent—yet we are plagued by violence. Recently, a child was caught in the crossfire of a gang dispute and was killed. Afterward, a TV news station featured several pastors saying how wretched people are and praying that we all would acknowledge our worthlessness so that God would forgive our sins.

What?

Some churches do not believe in the intrinsic worth of the people they are called to reach. Other churches tell us we are not responsible; everything is the devil's fault. We seem to have a deliverance center on every street corner. Every personal struggle is attributed to a demon.

I wager that no matter what programs are offered, until the Church changes her thinking about the worth of every person and focuses on our personal responsibility, we will not see much change. I am done hearing about another deliverance meeting. You would think we would be making some progress by now!

People are lost because of our stinking beliefs about who we are and whose we are. Our ability to shift the atmosphere over our own lives is crucial if we are going to shift the atmosphere over our workplaces, homes, or cities. The inability to shift my own atmosphere will limit my ability to see in the Spirit and to interact with the unseen realm, and it will keep me from pursuing all that God offers.

If you were wondering why there's a "worm" in this section heading, it's based on an old, macro belief system that we are all lowly sinners teetering on the brink of brimstone. Though none of us *really* think we are worms, that has been the dominant message in the Church for centuries. It has even been the basis for trying to get people into a relationship with Jesus. You could paraphrase the common evangelistic plea like this: "You are a lowly worm, but God loves you anyway, and you should be grateful about that."

Besides not being invitational, that belief messes with your discernment. If you believe you're a worm, you're going to discern like a worm, and you're going to discern everybody else's worminess. We end up reading someone and saying some version of, "I really feel their worminess." Remember, when we do that, we are simply manifesting on the outside what's going on inside us. Part of the training necessary to get past that happens within healthy leadership.

My wife is a prophet, and we lead together in our ministry, Building Contenders. She raises up other prophets and spearheads our prophetic training and our prophetic companies. When someone goofs with the prophetic, she has the job of correcting that person. This happened recently. A member of Rachel's team gave a public prophecy to someone during a church service, and the woman made a mistake. It wasn't deliberate, just a mistake.

I have to take a moment here and note that the Church can be really harsh on mistakes. Mistakes are not sins; mistakes are just mistakes. We're not dealing with a sin. And even when we are dealing with a sin, you are unpunishable. Not unaccountable, but unpunishable.

So back to the prophecy mistake. Rachel drew the woman alongside of her after church and said, "Hey, what do you think about that?" The team member said, "I'm sorry, I'll clean up my mess. What do I need to do to clean up my mess?"

At that moment, do you think trust was built or destroyed? Built, of course. Why? Because that team member has a teachable heart. She didn't get all defensive and weirdly over-spiritual, and not only did she own the mistake, she was willing to clean it up. You can call it submission, you can call it leadership, but this was a case of a humble leader connecting with a humble minister from the place of love.

As leaders, we haven't learned to govern well in humility and submission. As congregants, we haven't learned to approach each other and say, "Hey, I could be wrong on this, what do you think?"

Everyone must be teachable—leaders included. I am not a leader because I am the most gifted or powerful, I am a leader because God appointed me. My leaders are not in their positions because they served the longest in kids' church or swept the most floors. The leaders on my wife's prophetic team are not there because they have tenure at the church. They are there because we trust them.

Do you know how you destroy trust? Never admit that you are wrong and never admit you made a mistake.

I like to say that I give our church the great opportunity of following a leader who gets it wrong. A lot. Yes, I get things wrong. You're welcome. I make mistakes. Again, you're welcome. It is probably one of the hardest things perfectionist leaders get to do is to make mistakes and know that it affects a whole bunch of people.

I would suggest that no matter what prophetic or discerning word you get, you have to bring it under authority. And it's not your authority. Most church leaders, myself included, have not learned to govern well, and it is really hard for people to then submit to that governance well. Responsibility lies with both the minister and the leader. We *all* have a responsibility to create a system of honor.

To build trust, I have to admit when I am wrong. I can't make you trust me, and you can't make me trust you. Neither can we earn each other's trust. Trust has to be given, otherwise we are controlling a piece of someone else's heart.

And even if we fail miserably, we are not worms. We are children of a loving God who continually invites us to grow and learn with Him and with each other.

YOU HAVE AUTHORITY

Let's go a bit deeper into authority. In Matthew 8:5-13, we read the story of a centurion who asked Jesus to heal his servant. The centurion fully understood authority; he was under authority, and he had authority over people. He recognized Jesus as One with authority who didn't even need to come to his house or lay hands on the servant; He just needed to issue a command. And Jesus did. He said to the centurion, "Go; it shall be done for you as you have believed" (v 13 NASB). Jesus simply used His authority. As much as we balk at the word "authority," we must be submitted in our hearts to authority.

"You only have the authority that you're submitted to."
Equipped for Glory, Ian Carroll, Building Contenders. 2019

I suspect that everyone who has ever donned a uniform understands this principle; we operate under the authority of the one we submit to. By extension, we will also have the authority we are submitted to.

Did you know that you have authority over atmospheres? You can actually walk into a room and say to every foul spiritual force present that they are all subject to you because you have the Holy Spirit living inside of you, and those spirits don't get to influence you or your assignment. I've declared that aloud in my home, I've done it in church, I've done it in hospitals. I say aloud: "I speak to any foul spirit that's coming against the spirit of love, joy, peace, and I command you to go in Jesus' name."

A few years ago, I was in an airport in Orlando, Florida. I heard a woman scream for help. I saw that her infant was lying limp over her arms, not breathing. The woman was completely frantic. At the same time, a cloud of what smelled like death entered the area—that's the best way I can describe it. I stood and was filled with a spirit of boldness, and I began praying forcefully and audibly in tongues. I walked toward the cloud of death, and I felt a surge of power flow through me so mightily that I felt invincible. I began using my arms and my loud voice to push back on this cloud of death. At the very moment I reached the mother who was screaming and carrying her child, the child gasped and began breathing. The cloud disappeared. The medics arrived, and people looked at me as if I was crazy. Discerning the darkness was not the goal; conquering the darkness was.

I remember I was about to preach one Sunday during a difficult season in our church. When I reached the podium, I could see the spirit of religion walk into the sanctuary. Everyone was being really nice, probably feeling a little unsteady but putting their best foot forward, stirring up hope in the middle of a storm. When I saw the spirit of religion enter, I started making declarations. I don't even remember if I had the mic at that point, but I just started speaking out the goodness of God and our destiny as a church. I suspect that the evil spirit was going after people's vulnerability and wanted to turn good hearts to bitterness. When you make declarations, these foul things disappear. The demonic just starts to dissipate.

It reminds me of the scene in the film *Back To The Future* when Marty McFly is holding a photograph. Because of events currently happening, the old reality in the photograph starts to fade. That's how I imagine the demons start to fade when we start to declare the truth. At the same time, when we start to declare heaven's truth, the angels begin responding. They start to vibrate and hum like a tuning fork. It's called resonance. When things happen here on earth, they resonate in heaven.

Declarations are made continually in heaven. The angelic hosts never cease saying, "'Holy, holy, holy is the Lord God Almighty, who was, and is, and is to come'" (Revelation 4:8 NIV). Twenty-four elders respond to this never-ending declaration of worship by saying:

> You are worthy, our Lord and God, to receive glory and honor and power, for you

> created all things, and by your will they were created and have their being (Revelation 4:11 NIV).

Declarations of heaven's truth tap into the unseen realm, and we can experience the unseen becoming seen as we increase our faith and release the angelic. That is why our macro thinking is so very important.

Try this for a week. Meditate on your destiny. Imagine what it will look like when you stand in front of kings, when you play in front of thousands, or when you provide water for all those communities who have none. Imagine what it will look like, feel like, and be like when you are walking in the destiny you know God has planned for you.

When your macro beliefs include a good God who has good things for you, you know you have the authority to agree and declare that goodness in your life. And whatever your assignment, you have angels to help fulfill it, and you have the authority to empower those angels. Which leads us to the most popular element of the unseen, the angelic.

5: THE ANGELIC & DEMONIC

How can we interact with the angelic?
Is it important to study the demonic?
What's with all this "ranks of heaven" stuff?

I hear these kinds of questions often and don't have definitive answers. But I keep pressing into God, and I keep taking my faith to the *gymnazō*. Maybe some better questions to ask are: God, what is on your heart this minute? What can I learn that will help me partner with heaven?

Learning about the mystical realm is about *learning*. Training. Working it out. I don't know much about this realm. I do know that not all angels have feathery wings. I do know that the demonic exists and is active. And I do know that we should care about anything involving the Kingdom of God—and believe me: the angelic and demonic realms have everything to do with the Kingdom. But I will focus more on the angelic here because I like to keep my eyes on Jesus, not the devil. I'm plenty aware that the devil is active and at work; I just don't like to give him any special attention.

ANGELS & FAITH

Angels are everywhere in the Bible, including the New Testament. Angels scare the living daylights out of a bunch of shepherds in a field announcing the coming of Jesus. Angels prophesy to people, minister to Jesus, stir waters for healing, break people out of prison, and guard an empty tomb.

People often worry that a desire to encounter the angelic will turn into angel worship. That would be as dumb as making a golden calf and worshipping it. I hope it goes without saying that we don't pray to angels. We pray directly to God, who assigns the angels. We don't need an intermediary to connect with God, and God is more than big enough to handle whatever comes His way—or ours.

If you think like me, that then brings the question, "Can we command angels?" to mind. I dislike the word command. I do like the word cooperate. The apostle John certainly gave instructions to angels in the book of Revelation. Does that mean he is commanding them? Also, if Satan is some sort of heavenly being, can we take authority over him? I hope so, and in scripture, the process is simple. We submit to God and resist the devil. John is submitted to God and directing angels.

When we read about angelic encounters in Scripture, we discover that it can be difficult to differentiate between the presence of an angel and the presence of God Himself. In fact, angels often have to tell people to stop worshipping them. The sense of holiness that emanates from angels can feel so similar to God's holiness—at least to us—that it is easy to mistake. At times, God appears in the Old Testament as the Angel of the Lord, and He is worshipped appropriately.

Don't let fear keep you from growing your ability to interact with the angelic. If Jesus needed to be ministered to by angels, we should learn how to as well. Even if we aren't told what that actually looked like, we don't want fear to stop us from experimenting, learning, and growing.

Fear of deception will lead to policing our experience of the mystical realm, which will limit the revelation we can receive. The Old and New Testaments are filled with revelation from angels. If angels appeared to Daniel and Mary, they can appear to us.

And if they do appear, what is our responsibility? Let's look at the passage in John that describes the healing of the man at the Pool of Bethesda:

> Now there is in Jerusalem by the sheep gate a pool, which is called in Hebrew Bethesda, having five porticoes. In these lay a multitude of those who were sick, blind, lame, and withered, (waiting for the moving of the waters; for an angel of the Lord went down at certain seasons into the pool and stirred up the water; whoever then first, after the stirring up of the water, stepped in was made well from whatever disease with which he was afflicted.) A man was there who had been ill for thirty-eight years. When Jesus saw him lying there, and knew that he had already been a long time in that condition, He said to him, "Do you wish to get well?" The sick man answered Him, "Sir, I have no man to put me into the pool when the water is stirred up, but while I am coming, another steps down before me." Jesus said to him, "Get up, pick up your pallet and walk." Immediately the man became well, and picked up his pallet and [began] to walk... (John 5:4-9, NASB).

Note that the appearance of the angel didn't reduce the responsibility of the sick man. The sick man still had to get up, he still had to make his way to the water, and he still had to be the first in. Even though the angel made it possible, he didn't make it easy. God likes to work *with* us, and *with* requires participation.

It's important enough to repeat: the appearance of the angel did not reduce the personal responsibility of the sick man. In fact, Jesus healed the man by giving him instructions to get up, pick up his mat, and walk.

This is also important enough to repeat: angels aren't here to make everything easy breezy. They don't magically wave a wand and make our problems disappear. That is just a fantasy—a misinformed desire to live a life devoid of faith. Faith requires something from us. The goal of seeing the unseen is not to remove doubt. It is not to have certainty so that we no longer need faith.

I should mention here that there is such a thing as "dead faith." This is the kind of "faith" that says, "I am waiting on God." If someone tells me he has faith but he is just waiting on God to open a door, I would argue that he either doesn't have faith or he has dead faith, because faith without works is dead. Dead! Ceased to be! *True* faith requires action. James 2:20 tells us that faith requires "works." The Greek word for "works" in that passage is *ergon*. It literally means to work at something, to do stuff. Passivity nullifies faith. I could paraphrase that passage in James by saying, "True faith requires hope in action."

Waiting on God to give us the ability to see in the Spirit is not faith. In fact, that inaction requires zero faith. Like everything else in life, we need to break the passive nature (which the enemy really enjoys) and start changing our thinking and changing our behavior to obtain the gifts God has for us.

What if God wants us to experience the unseen with Him? What would you do if you knew you had access to seeing in the Spirit? What actions would you take to experience more of what heaven is doing on earth?

The sick man by the Pool of Bethesda had been waiting for his healing for 38 years. When Jesus asked him if he wanted to get well, he did not answer Jesus' question. In self-pity, he basically said, "It's not my fault I haven't been healed, I don't have anybody to help me." Jesus felt compassion for the man, and His solution was to tell the man to get up.

Assuming a victim role will stop you from engaging with the angelic in your life. It will prevent you from reaping the benefits that come with a divinely sent minister who is with you to fulfill your assignment. Being a passive agent in your own life may even open you up to darker ministers who are intent on you *not* becoming who God has ordained you to be. This man's inability to shift the atmosphere over his own life, the atmosphere that grew through sickness and 38 years of disappointment and pain, had prevented him from receiving his healing. Later, Jesus met him and told him not to return to a sinful life, or something worse might happen. Since we know the character of God as a Good Father, that "something worse" would not be an assignment from heaven but an assignment from hell based on the foothold the man had been giving to the enemy.

RANK & ORDER

The Kingdom of God is a Kingdom of order, and this applies to the angelic realm as well. In a world of participation trophies, we might resent hierarchy, but it's a spiritual fact. I would go so far as to say that any understanding of authority that doesn't understand hierarchy is misleading. Heaven *does* have rank and order.

Some people who go to heaven say they see mellow pastoral fields, and everything is all green and pleasant. I've had experiences like that, but most of the times I go to heaven, I encounter more of a metropolitan feel—almost industrial and highly productive; there is a lot going on.

On one visit, I remember thinking, "Wow—this place is really, really loud!" There was so much activity and worship and glory it was almost over-stimulating, but it was very much in order.

So, let's dig into the historical perspective of the order of heaven and the ranks of angels within that. Much of this is from Thomas Aquinas, one of the pillars of the Catholic Church. He worked long and hard on his book, the *Summa Theologica*, but when he had an encounter with God, he said that all his studies were like vapor in comparison to the encounter he had with the Father. It is a good reminder that it's wonderful to learn and study, but it's even better to connect with the One we're studying.

THE THREE HEAVENS

Though Aquinas is right about an encounter with God being even better than studying God, I do think that the study of heaven and the angelic can help us by increasing our awareness of God's plans and purposes—and how we can partner with them. So let's take a quick look at the three heavens and the angelic beings within each of them. One thing to note: there is a constant mood of adoration of God in all three of these heavens.

THIRD HEAVEN

The third heaven is the top of the hierarchy, and the highest angelic beings in this realm are the seraphim. "Seraphim" is literally translated as "burning ones." They serve as caretakers for the throne room of God, and they are continually shouting praise: *Holy, holy, holy*. You can hear this praise in heaven; it is like a heartbeat. In Isaiah 6, the seraphim are described as fiery, six-winged beasts. Two wings cover their faces, another two cover their feet, and with the last two wings they fly. They are impressive beings.

The next level of angelic beings in the third heaven are the cherubim. They have four faces: one of a man, an ox, a lion, and an eagle. They have four conjoined wings covered with eyes (although the Book of Revelation describes them with six wings, almost like the seraphim). Cherubim have a lion's body and the feet of oxen—this is no feathery being holding a sword. In Genesis, we read that they were appointed to guard the way to the tree of life in the Garden of Eden, and in Ezekiel we read that they are in the throne room of God as well. One of my pet peeves is the depiction of cherubim as chubby little baby angels. Those are *not* cherubim according to Scripture. The chubby baby angels you see depicted in Renaissance art are called *putti*, and they appear nowhere in Scripture. Like the seraphim, the cherubim are mighty and impressive: no baby fat.

After the seraphim and cherubim come the thrones or elders. Colossians 1:6 describes Jesus being above all thrones: those thrones are actually spiritual entities. They are also called elders. These beings are casting their crowns before the feet of God. In traditional angelology, the thrones/elders are symbols of God's justice and authority, hence the symbol of the throne.

SECOND HEAVEN

In this second realm, heavenly beings are governing creation. They are also in charge of other angelic beings. First of these are the dominions (sometimes referred to as lordships). Say "dominions" in a contemporary charismatic church, and it's probably a reference to the dark version. In fact, the dark dominions are counterfeits of the real ones—the angelic or heavenly dominions. The dominions' job is to regulate or manage the lower angels. I think I've seen dominions at a distance, but I don't think I've ever met one. Tradition says they look like really beautiful humans, but they do have wings and do carry symbols of governance like scepters.

The next level of angelic beings in the second heaven is that of the strongholds. Similar to dominions, we often think of strongholds as the bad version—the things that we have to break off or cast down and all that. One of the many useful parts of Aquinas's work in describing these realms was to also call the strongholds "virtues." The strongholds—or virtues—make a way for miracles, signs, and wonders from the second heaven to reach earth. Strongholds are often associated with the Greek word *dunamis*, or power, and they seem to have a certain unshakeable, fortified quality which helps them release heaven's miraculous agenda.

Then comes the third rank in the Second Heaven: powers or authorities. These are more associated with the Greek word *exousia*, or authority. The powers/authorities are all about order, and they are the warriors. They are going after the enemy and fighting battles in the heavenly realm. They are often represented wearing armor and wielding swords, chains, and weapons. They are fiercely loyal to God. Tradition holds that none of these powers fell with Satan. Because of their fierce loyalty to the King and the Kingdom, none of them ever rebelled. I just love that. Part of the heavenly order they establish is from heaven to earth. And these angelic beings distribute power to humans.

FIRST HEAVEN

The highest-ranking officials in the first heaven are called principalities or rulers. Their job is to protect nations and groups of people. A principality can encompass a geographical or even a demographic region. These heavenly beings might protect a group of churches, a city, a region, or a country. Principalities or rulers are often seen wearing a crown and carrying either a scepter or an orb.

The second in rank in the first heaven is the archangel. The word is used only twice in the New Testament: 1 Thessalonians 4:16 and Jude 1:9. The only archangel ever mentioned by name in the New Testament is Michael. Most Christian traditions also include Gabriel as an archangel, and in Jewish traditions, there are a couple more. But the word archangel only appears as a singular noun in Scripture—never plural. In non-cannon writings, we also have the appearance of Raphael, who is mentioned as an archangel. More to the point: an archangel is a general. The assignment of the archangel is to disperse authority and power and to make sure that the rest of the angels are doing what they are assigned to do.

Finally, the lowest rank is in the first heaven is the angels. These are the beings we are most familiar with because their role is to be concerned with living things. We are so interested in them because they are the ones we most often encounter. I believe that the angels are primarily here to help us accomplish the assignments we have been given from higher angelic beings.

Instead of more description here, I'll tell you some of my experience with angels.

SOME ANGEL ENCOUNTERS

My good friend, Jennifer Eivaz, wrote a book called *The Intercessors Handbook*. In it, she describes me as having an unusual relationship with the angelic. I remember the first time she published an excerpt from the book on The Elijah List mentioning this. I was horrified. For years, I have avoided being labeled as the angel guy. I have kept quiet about what I see. In all my years of preaching in my current church, I have spoken maybe four times on the angelic. I have resisted my ability to see more than I have embraced it.

A couple of months ago, I was challenged about this resistance by my friend Keith Ferrante, a prophet in Vacaville, California. We were talking about some growing opportunities I have had as an apostle. Over the last year or so, I have had the privilege of speaking into the life and government of some churches in the region. My influence is small, but I feel so honored to be invited by men and women of God to come to their churches and give wisdom and input where it is sought.

Keith told me it was time to go public with my stories and that God would open doors and begin ministering to all those outside the Church who have similar experiences but no context. So, my days of resistance are over. If I am known as the angel man, so be it. If I am considered weird, so be it. Here it goes...

***

In the prologue, I mentioned my days at a Belfast city mission. At that time, there was a group of mystics among us—

mostly hippies who dropped a lot of LSD in their days before Jesus. They talked in transcendent ways about music, God, books, Scripture, and love. Through one of them, I began opening up to the unseen realm. His name is Terry Hogg, and the first time I heard him speak was at one of our weekend retreats. I still remember his sermon called "The Lord of the Ring". I was inspired and bought the entire Tolkien series of books, which remain my all-time favorites.

Terry helped us understand that the Holy Bible was more than a road map to heaven. It was at once knowable and unknowable. It was real and mystical. The words in it weren't just good for memorization and instruction, but were also God-breathed. The Word is living, and it is a tool to equip us for every good work and to advance the Kingdom. (And if believing in a book that has been breathed on by God Himself is not mystical, I don't know what is!)

At the time, I was reading a lot of A.W. Tozer. At the back of his books, I discovered lists of books by old mystics, and I would try to read them to understand some of the experiences I was having.

Experiences like lying on my bed with my eyes open and seeing myself walk to church. In a vision, I would see someone leave his house, get into his blue car, and drive off. I would walk into church and meet a specific person who would say a specific thing. Thirty minutes later, as I was walking to church in the natural, I would experience 80% of what I had seen in my vision. Weird! I had no grid for this, and no one to talk to about it, so I just filed it away in my mind.

In 1987, I was baptized in the Holy Spirit. A few months later, I began speaking in tongues. The awareness and closeness of God during this time was something I had sought but not experienced until then. Along with it came an awareness of the demonic. I would be patrolling the streets and see things that would curl your hair. Foul, evil beasts of all kinds, none of them born in this seeing world.

Around 1990, I started participating in deliverance ministries that helped people involved in the occult. Covens across Ireland began praying against me. Nasty things appeared in my bedroom which my newlywed wife could feel but thankfully not see. I have no interest in describing these things in detail. I'll just say I was under attack.

Then, Jesus showed up during a deliverance meeting. I don't mean in that goosebumps way we think of during worship. I mean He walked into the room where we were trying to deliver a guy from his demons. After that, the attacks stopped.

In 1994, I was at another church. Some of our elders had been on a secret recon trip to a little church by an airport in

Toronto to see what all the fuss was about. Let's just say that when they returned: I got blasted by the Toronto Blessing. I fell to the floor and laughed for over an hour. I got up and felt a little drunk, but like the disciples in Acts 2, I was not drunk as you might suppose.

My experiences with the unseen realm were about to explode.

***

One of my colleagues at the time had committed his life to Satan. It was a deliberate decision he had made at a time of crisis when he felt God had not come through for him. He knew he had demons and was actually quite proud of them. One of his demons was a spirit of division. He would tell me that he was aware of the fact that I was filled with the Holy Spirit, not like those other nominal, evangelical Christians. I would tell him he was full of nonsense, and I would not be listening to a demon—especially one trying to separate believers and bring disunity.

This man was a detective and was pretty good at it. He was able to discover suspects' secrets—likely passed from their demons to his. He would often freak out suspects with his knowledge of their lives.

Despite all that, I liked this guy, and I longed for him to be free. The day after I got blasted by the Holy Spirit, I went to work. I walked into the building where his office was. From his desk, he saw me coming, and he was all smiles as usual—for a split second. Then he looked like he had seen something terrifying, stood up, and bolted toward the back door saying in a loud voice, "I don't like this! I don't like this!"

He stood a room's distance away from me and asked me in a feverish tone, "What have you done? What happened? I don't like this." So, I told him. He was never the same around me. He could not stand the presence of God. I knew that something had changed in me, and I would never be the same.

***

Not long after that, I started going into deep trances, quite literally falling off my chair onto the ground and "going places" to talk with Jesus. I would "return" to the regular world, thinking I had been "out" for 10 or 15 minutes, when, in fact, it had been two or three hours.

Then, I started to see angels. Everywhere. I would drive to work and see cars with angels sitting on the roofs. I would be in church listening to the sermon, and an angel would appear on stage with the preacher. One time, I was listening to the prophet, Sharon Stone, prophesying over a man. As she was speaking, I saw angels fly from her mouth, go to the man, and lay hands on him.

Sometimes during worship, I would become simply overwhelmed by the numbers of angels and the volume of noise they were making. I didn't know what to do. I mean, what *do* you do? I hadn't learned how to interact with the mystical realm. I didn't know if we should stop the meeting and see why they were there—and I didn't exactly want to admit to what I was seeing in the first place! I had no clue and no one to ask.

***

Years and years went by, and I still didn't know what to do with all of my experiences. Then, I went to heaven for the first time in January 2008. I was attending a conference at what was then called Toronto Airport Christian Fellowship, now Catch the Fire Church. This was the very place my previous church elders had gone and brought back that fire that propelled me on my mystical journey.

I was in a line to be prayed for and decided I wouldn't wait to fall down (I usually fall forwards, and "catchers" are generally unprepared for this), so I laid down on the floor, and someone from the ministry team prayed for me. I sensed the Holy Spirit moved through me like electricity and heard His voice asking me if I wanted to come with Him. I was a little afraid but said *yes*. An angel came, took me by the hand, and in an instant, I stood in front of a building.

I have never seen anything as big as this building. It was vast. Architecturally, it was a mixture of ancient and futuristic, both ornate and simple. It was constructed of some kind of stone that glowed in the light. The noise was deafening, but not threatening. In the distance, a huge party was gathered, and the atmosphere was electric with anticipation.

The angel asked me if I wanted to see my storeroom, and, of course, I said *yes*. Again, he took my hand, and I was at once inside a room that was heavy with history. I can remember the smell; it smelled how you would imagine the color yellow to smell: bright, summery, and new. I was shown racks of what looked like clothes and shelves filled with equipment I have never seen before and wouldn't know how to describe. The room was crammed with weapons, machines, books, oils, pens, and technology.

A voice—I don't know if it was the angel or not—asked me, "What are you waiting for? You have been equipped with everything you need."

In an instant, I was back on the carpet in Toronto. Afterward, I shared this with Rachel. She had experienced a separate encounter very similar to mine. We knew that the time was now, but we were unclear of the meaning and thought it may mean moving. Little did I know that, in less than six months, I would become the senior pastor of my church and begin leading. Thankfully, I had already been equipped, as promised.

***

A few months later, I was lying on my bed asking God for the strategy to win our city of Chicago. I asked the Father if He would show me His plan, and in an instant, I stood in the strategy room of heaven. Before me lay a map of the greater Chicago area. Angels were floating around the map focused on it. I looked at it, too. Different places were lit up; some were super bright, some were super dim, and others were flickering between light and dim.

I asked about the lights. One of the angels, who held an object that moved the lights around the map, answered that the lights were churches walking in their assignments. Some lights glowed brightly, some were dim, and some had gone out altogether. Now and then, the map changed its angle ever so slightly, and the lights shifted. Some would move entirely, and others would get brighter. Again, a voice spoke and said, "The strategy for your city is that you be known as people marked by My presence and known by your love for each other."

And then I was back on my bed. For the next few years, that strategy held us together as a team and as a church. We have pursued His presence and are still growing in our love for each other.

***

I have three angels who often travel with me. One of them has been with me since 2008, and his name is Valor. He almost always stands to my left, and he is very protective of me. One part of my calling is to encourage people that impossible things are possible. The anointing for this comes from the Father and is supported by an angel who knows how to persevere in a fight.

Another angel, Breakthrough, is...how can I say this? Well, you wouldn't look at him and think: *Wow, he's a super beautiful angel!* Breakthrough appeared the other day as I was traveling to speak because that event was all about breakthrough. He increases and decreases in size based on what's being pulled from him. If people are pulling for breakthrough, he will respond by increasing. He isn't a massive being waiting to smash and demolish walls. He carries a kind of club on a very short chain. When he swings it, it will go through a wall—but it pierces through the wall and breaks it down one brick at a time. Sometimes, breakthrough happens one brick at a time; sometimes, God gives you your promised land one bit at a time because if He gives you the whole thing at once, your enemies are going to overrun you.

Then there's another angel called Faith. His personality is completely different from the other two. I've come to really respect him and admire him. I first met him in the Maldives five years ago. He came to hang out on the outside deck of where we were staying, with a group of angels. They would laugh and roar and have a great ol' time. It's like they were drunk—but not drunk as you might suppose: drunk in the goodness of God. They started telling stories of breakthrough and stories of testimony. Things like, "Do you remember when they thought that child was dead but God brought him back to life?" They told stories about how God intervened in our human paths and messes. I got to have a conversation with Faith afterward, and he said, "I was there on Mother's Day, 1980." That was the day the Holy Spirit broke out in the Vineyard Anaheim. He said, "All my time as an angel, I've been assigned to movements." Extraordinary.

***

Recently, I was preparing for my Sunday sermon when my angel Valor came to my room and asked if I wanted to go with him. Of course I did! He took me by the hand, and we went to heaven and sat on a hill overlooking the throngs of streets and buildings around the throne room.

He simply asked me one question: "What do you experience as the atmosphere in heaven?" It was nothing short of jubilant expectation. In our pursuit of seeing the fulfilment of Jesus' prayer that earth be like heaven, it is helpful to experience the atmosphere of heaven—which is radically at odds with the atmosphere of the media we are bombarded with through TV and the internet. God really cares for the hurting, the wounded, and the beaten down. He will one day make everything more than better, and all of heaven is joyfully expectant of that day.

***

There is so much mystery in the mystical realm. It's no coincidence those two words share the same root.

One night after a church gathering, I was driving back home at about one or two in the morning. All of a sudden, a chariot pulled out in front of me. I slammed on my brakes.

"Jesus!?" I asked, "what was that about?"

"Oh, it's just for fun."

"Um, OK...."

He has a sense of humor. That encounter reminded me that we can't get religious about the mystical realm. It can be serious, but not religious. In fact, I've met very serious angels.

One had an English accent. Another stays in our house. He looks like he is from the Middle East, and he walks around our house reading a book. If you walk into a room where he is, he gets up and leaves. He doesn't like being in the same room as any of us. Sometimes, when I'm sitting in my living room, he'll be coming down the stairs reading a book. When he sees me, he'll turn around and go back upstairs. Mystery.

I've met angels with very strong personalities, and I've met angels with slightly grumpy personalities. Valor has a really good personality. He's really bubbly and friendly. He'll show up in the back of our car and ask, "What's happening? What's going on? Are we going anywhere nice?" On our way to the Maldives for our 25th anniversary, we flew into Dubai. I didn't see Valor around in the airport, and I thought he was just giving us some time alone. All of a sudden, he was standing right beside me saying, "I've never been to Dubai before. This place is amazing!" Mystery.

***

In the middle of the night years ago, I was awakened by a man standing beside my bed. I was startled, but not afraid. I recognized him as Larry Randolph, a well-known prophet and leader of Larry Randolph Ministries. I have never met him in person; I just knew who he was. My wife was sleeping beside me in bed, undisturbed. Larry woke me and told me he was there to deliver a message to me and that because of the importance of the message, it was being done in an unusual way. He told me, "God has appointed you as an apostle." Then he blessed me and left. It was all pretty matter of fact.

***

I try to go hiking in Yosemite once a year. One time, I started hiking at around 4 AM for the long trek up to a place called Clouds Rest. When I reached the summit, I was the only one there. Immediately, I could see a lot of angelic activity in the skies, so I sat, prayed, and watched.

As people started to arrive, I decided to walk down a bit and have lunch. I found a spot where I could lie on a rock and worship. As I prayed, God asked me if I would like to see everything that was going on. Of course, I said *yes*. From the bottom right of my view, He seemed to grab the corner of a screen, peeling it away and up toward the left, revealing the unseen realm. I sat in awe for over an hour watching.

I've mentioned that it can be difficult to describe the unseen. I'd like to expand on that a bit for a moment.

In the book of Revelation, John describes a lot of strange things. In Chapter 4 for example, he tells us that there are four living creatures sitting before the throne. One is *like* a lion, one *like* a calf, one with a face *like* a man, and the fourth *like* a flying eagle. They all have six wings, covered with eyes all around. Leaving aside the symbolism and metaphors of what he is describing, I want you to think about the difficulty of describing something you have no context for. How do I describe a color that does not exist in the seen realm but exists in the unseen? How do I describe seeing something that looks like it is a man but also like a lion and a lamb? When we see something, there are three components; the revelation, the interpretation, and the application. These are really useful when seeing the unseen.

Some folks seem to easily see, describe, and interpret things, like: "A blue angel just appeared on your right. It is here to give you authority for revelation." They have seen something and can immediately interpret it based on what they have come to understand; blue is for revelation and being on the right gives authority and favor. They can even use that seeing experience as a launch pad for more prophetic revelation. Sometimes, that happens to me. But most times? Not so much. I see the unseen with more awe than understanding. But I continue to ask for interpretation, and I continue to learn.

When I released my first book, *As It Is In Heaven*, people stood in line waiting for me to sign it. While waiting, many of them flipped to the chapter on angels and started to read it right away. There is such a hunger for things of the Spirit. Yet, there is a disparity between what we experience but aren't aware of and what we're aware of but aren't experiencing. As that disparity becomes greater and greater, we can become more disappointed and begin to wonder if any of it is really true.

In *As It Is In Heaven*,[2] I described how I saw the angel of Chicago enter a meeting:

> Jesus Culture, a ministry started at Bethel Church, Redding, came to Chicago in August 2011. On the last night of the event, something amazing happened. Banning Liebscher went on stage to close worship and transition into ministry. At least he tried to. As he began to speak, there was a massive influx of angels. Some people near me felt something brushing against them. I had never seen anything like it. The angels were manic—flying, looping the looping, swarming. Then the congregation continued in spontaneous worship, in what sounded like a Native American chant. People were on their feet giving glory to Jesus, and sud-

2 You can find that book on my website: www.buildingcontenders.com.

> denly the angels gathered, created an open space in their midst, and fell into lines like an army. When they made space, in came the angel of Chicago. He was massive. The worship intensified even more, and this angel, bigger than any I have ever seen, fell to his knees, a signal that every other angel followed. And in came Jesus. King Jesus in all His splendor entered the Allstate Arena, and the place erupted with worship once more! I was undone.

Allstate Arena is big. It seats over 16,000 people, and that night it was pretty full. I have no idea how many angels were present, but the number was in the tens of thousands. Also, the angel of Chicago was way bigger than the arena itself, yet it looked like he fit inside the arena along with the thousands of angels.

When Jesus came in, he dwarfed everyone. He made even the largest angels seem small. As I try to describe this, I can't come close. That is part of the problem with seeing; it usually doesn't make sense, and it never fits into any box of human logic. Seers end up trying to use metaphors to make sense of things. We just do our best, and we practice discernment.

LOOK FOR THE GOOD

A key to understanding the angelic and demonic is discernment, which we looked at in Chapter 3. Our gift of discernment has to operate in a way that we see more of heaven than anything else.

In other words, if you are seeing more of the demonic than the angelic, you need to readjust your focus. Whatever we focus on, we cultivate in our lives. So, I have no idea why anyone would focus on the demonic. I want to see Jesus. I want to see His face. I want to see His hands. I want to see all that He is doing in my family, my church, and this earth. I want to see what Jesus and His angels are doing more than what the enemy and his demons are doing.

Jesus is not reactive; He is proactive. We need to switch our thinking: we aren't to be worried that the enemy is coming after us; we are to be advancing the Kingdom of God—and swiping at the enemy when he gets in the way. Like Jesus, we are proactively bringing heaven to earth. To do that, we must be able to see in the spirit realm, the realm of heaven.

As I mentioned earlier, we have misunderstood discernment by thinking its purpose is to detect evil. It's probably a really bad idea to think that a gift of the Holy Spirit is for the purpose of discovering the works of the devil. In fact, if we believe that, we might just be blaspheming the Holy Spirit. Let's not attribute the life-giving abilities of the Holy Spirit to the destructive abilities of the devil. The gift of discernment is for discerning good from evil and engaging with the good.

Don't get me wrong, I believe in demons, and I have seen them. But they only have access to our lives if we give them access. That's why I'm barely addressing them in this chapter—and not even giving them their own subheading.

Our beliefs, attitudes, and behaviors will attract the unseen realm, for better or for worse. We have the choice to focus on what heaven is doing and to train our gift of sight to see it happen on earth.

6: EXERCISE YOUR FAITH

Many years ago, I was seeking the gift of tongues. Someone gave me a tiny booklet describing a person's experience of receiving the gift. I read that they had lain down on the floor with arms outstretched, asked for the gift of tongues, and then the Spirit fell on them. They experienced what seemed like an uncontrollable gift of language.

So I tried it. I spread out on the floor and waited to be overtaken by the Spirit. I was expecting Him to just take over my larynx and breath, and then the words would come out. That didn't happen. What happened was that months later, I was in a worship service. At one point, there was a crescendo in praise, and everyone was calling out to Jesus. I thought I was shouting, along with everyone else, that He was King of Kings, He was worthy, He was Holy. But as the noise level decreased, I heard myself actually singing in an unknown tongue. I immediately stopped.

The awareness of what I was doing was enough to make me doubt that it was the gift of tongues. But I kept experimenting. Truthfully, for months, I felt I was simply making it up. There was no ecstatic sense of being taken over. I just blabbered as quickly as I could. A dear friend suggested I take a deep breath and slow the whole thing down. As I practiced, things shifted. My awareness shifted from myself and centered on Him. My gift began growing, like a muscle; I was going to the *gymnazō*. I was exercising my faith.

When I ask people about their experience receiving the gift of tongues, most of them had also expected it to just "land" on them without them doing anything. Like me, they felt like they were making it up at first. That common misconception stems from being taught that there is no action required of us—that every gift of the Spirit just comes to us. The opposite is true.

Scripture tells us to eagerly desire things of the Spirit. 1 Corinthians 14:39 calls readers to eagerly desire the gift of prophecy. What is translated in the NIV as "eagerly desire" (in other translations as "earnestly desire") is the Greek word *zēloō*. It means to burn with zeal, to actively pursue. This is no passive desire; it is a jealousy for, a burning for, a pursuit.

All of the gifts require us to pursue them. The same goes for seeing in the Spirit. Instead of starting at point A, most people who begin training their gift want to automatically jump to point Z and experience everything that seasoned seers experience. God is too good to let that happen.

If we go to the gym and just start lifting heavy weights before we've built up the muscles to handle them, we will get injured. We have to train. We start by lifting smaller weights and working on our form. We do the reps. We grow. As with a physical workout, we can grow the gifts of the Spirit at our own pace and the level of our desire.

SPIRITUAL PRINCIPLES

God gives us gifts. It's up to us to partner with Him to increase those gifts. This works for most everything, from finances to receiving a prophet to impartation. When you sow money into a ministry serving the Kingdom, you partner with God to see increase come from the seed you have sown. If you receive a prophet in the name of a prophet, you get a prophet's reward. If you have a gift or grace on your life, you increase it by imparting it onto someone else. These are all acts of faith. And these are also spiritual principles.

We are constantly working with spiritual principles—good and bad. Many of our problems actually stem from wrong spiritual principles, aligned with politics and religion rather than the Kingdom. We live in both the material and the mystical realm, simultaneously. What we build in the mystical realm, we can also build in the material realm. (In the Western world, we may need to explain the mystical or spiritual realm, simply because so much of it has been hijacked.)

When the Apostle Paul talks about spiritual things, he's not talking about the twenty-first-century notion of being "spiritual"—that "I'm not religious, I'm spiritual" kind of thing. The Apostle Paul uses the word spiritual *always* in relation to the Holy Spirit. For example, in 1 Corinthians 2:15, he writes: "But he who is spiritual appraises all things..." (NASB). The word for "appraises" there is "judges" in other translations, which can make things confusing, but my focus here is on the word "spiritual." In this context, Paul is actually saying that whoever is filled with the Holy Spirit appraises all things. This isn't lowercase spiritual, it's capital-S Spiritual—Holy-Spiritual, if you will.

Each year in Chicago, something terrible happens. The first snowfall hits us, and it seems like the entire driving population forgets how to drive. People are unsure whether to brake hard, speed up going around corners, take off from a standing stop with great speed, or whatever. They forget the principles of driving they learned in previous years. Just like Chicago drivers (don't get me started on Southern Californian drivers when it rains!), we risk learning principles and later forgetting them in the days of sunshine and peace.

As important as it is to learn and train in spiritual principles, they should never take the place of the spiritual relationship we have with the Holy Spirit. Relationship always comes before principles. The mystical realm is weird and exciting, but it should never become more exciting than your personal relationship with God.

And the mystical realm doesn't take the place of miracles, signs, and wonders; it is fused with them. Heal the sick, raise the dead, cleanse the leper, set people free from their demons—that's our mandate. That brings the Kingdom, and bringing the Kingdom is our focus. Our job is to get the hell out of the earth. The mystical realm opens the way to miracles, signs, and wonders which point to the God who loves us.

Our job is to exercise our faith to see what God is up to and to partner with it to further His Kingdom.

7: QUESTIONS

Over the years, I've been asked many questions about the mystical realm—and I've asked many myself. In this chapter, I've gathered some of those questions, and I've responded not so much with answers as ideas—and more questions. These are things I have learned, wondered about, or experienced. They are in no way definitive, but I hope they will be helpful.

WHERE AND WHAT IS HEAVEN?

Many of us have been taught that heaven is the placid place we go to in the sky when we die. Once there, we will sit on a cloud playing a harp, waiting for the worship service to begin.

Please, please, please don't send me to that boring place!

Heaven is the place where Jesus is going to rule and reign—and where we are going to rule and reign *with* Him. What if it is a place where we actually partner with Him to see the goodness of God grow and to see the increase of His government and of His peace...here on earth? On earth as it is in heaven. What if the realm of heaven isn't just "up there" in the clouds, but right here on earth? What if it is the mystical realm we are learning to see?

HOW DO WE INCREASE HIS KINGDOM & PEACE?

Of the increase of His government and of His peace, there should be no end. So...are we partnering with God to increase His government and His peace? Are we doing like Jesus did? Are we thinking and acting from a place of divine power or from a victim mindset? Are we creating unity or division?

Every. Single. Thought. Every single thought we think is either working to increase His government and His peace... or the opposite. And since our thoughts form our actions, we have a mighty responsibility to be thinking from heaven to earth.

The kingdom of darkness has the goal of chaos. You can see it on the streets, you can feel it in the airwaves. Media is driven by it. Our job to counteract these principalities and powers does not seem to be shouting at territorial entities. Our power comes by bringing every thought into captivity, to bring the peace of heaven into our lives and experience it. By doing this, we manifest a different Kingdom.

We *must* have a victorious mindset. If we're just seeing things and circumstances as they appear to be—unvictorious—then we're looking at them from earth to heaven. It's a matter of re-aligning our thinking to heaven's reality. The *real* reality.

AM I MAKING THIS UP?

As you start to see things in the spirit, I can almost guarantee that you're going to start wondering if you're making it up. What about the flickers in your peripheral vision? Or something that flashes before you? Unless you're super special, most everyone starts his seer journey thinking, "Well, that was just me. Or a floater in my eye." We get the gift of tongues, and we think we're faking it—that's what I thought when I received the gift.

Here's my counsel to you: so what if you are? Has anybody died? Nope. Have you learned something? Probably. Are you pressing in and asking God what He's doing? I hope so. And if you do, you're learning. You're training.

We can't remain frustrated and fearful about the mystical realm because it's all about Jesus and heaven…which are all about peace and goodness. As you figure things out, I highly recommend this deceptively simple wisdom from Psalm 46:10 "Be still, and know that I am God" (NIV). I like that the translator put a comma after "still." It's like an extra pause—an implied "take a breath." We usually need to not just be still physically, but mentally, too. We need to quiet our thoughts. And then we remember what we know, we have a good God.

ARE GHOSTS REAL?

What are ghosts? People claim to have seen them, but Christian theology doesn't seem to make room for them. What if "ghosts" are actually lingering memories of a person or a place? We've seen that our thoughts create realities. What if memories are not just ideas that exist in our mind? And when traumatic events occur, what if some of that trauma remains in the land—in the place where it occurs—that we remember/think about? What if the land remembers?

Spooky, I know. But the Bible is full of trauma remaining in the land. The blood of Abel cried out from the ground; did the memory of that traumatic incident on the land affect that piece of land? I don't know.

When it says in Romans 8 that all of creation is groaning for the manifestation of the children of God, do we actually believe that it's groaning? Maybe it's just metaphorical. But maybe not…

CAN WE TALK TO THE DEAD?

Here's a question: what if you don't die and you just go to be with Jesus? Did I freak you out? I'm not questioning the "be with Jesus" part, but what I am questioning is what we think of the "death" part. What if we don't technically die? What if we simply step into life with Jesus in a different realm? And if so, those we thought had "died" and gone to be with Jesus aren't actually dead; they are in the cloud of witnesses of Heaven. So maybe we *can* talk to them…

Jesus talked to people we would have called dead. He spoke to Elijah and Moses. You might say, "Well, Elijah didn't die. He was transfigured or caught up into the Heavens." OK, but Moses was inarguably dead. Joshua 1:2 straight up says, "Moses, my servant, is dead" (NIV). It reminds me of the Monty Python sketch when a customer tries to convince a pet shop clerk that the parrot he just purchased is dead: "This parrot is no more! He has ceased to be! 'E's expired and gone to meet 'is maker! 'E's a stiff! Bereft of life, 'E rests in peace!"[3]

---

3 From the Monty Python script, "Dead Parrot." http://montypython.50webs.com/scripts/Series_1/53.htm

Basically, Moses had crossed over...and yet Jesus talked with him. So, is that a precedent for "talking to the dead"? Maybe.

I don't think we should seek out the dead, but what happens when the dead seek us? If it happens, bring it under authority. Keep your discernment on full alert. Make sure that God is in it. And He can be.

But—there is always a "but"—we probably need some protocols. We probably don't want to go looking for a spirit guide to take us to talk to the dead. That's anti-Bible. But within the mystical realm, there might be times when you find yourself seeing or being aware of people who are with Jesus.

Let's be cautious, but let's not miss out on anything that God wants to do.

CAN THE CLOUDS OF WITNESS VISIT US?

Days before she died, my mom called me. She said, "Son, I just want to know: are you happy?"

I answered, "I am."

She asked, "Are you doing what He wants you to do?"

And I said, "I am."

And she said, "OK."

That was the last conversation I had with my mom. Rachel and I lived 4,000 miles away, and we had spent the last number of years not seeing our parents. I grieved, but I also knew that my mom was—is—cheering me on in Heaven. I know she is part of the great cloud of witnesses and that they are not dead. They're right beside Jesus.

I have been in meetings when people from the great cloud of witnesses have walked in. Last year in California, a group of prophets had gathered together. I leaned over to Rachel and said, "Bob Jones just walked into the room."

Bob Jones was a prophet who went to be with the Lord a few years ago. About ten minutes after I saw Bob, the prophetic intercessor got up, and said the great cloud of witnesses were coming and were excited about what God was doing. Afterward, I went over to the intercessor and asked him, "Were you talking about Bob Jones?"

He said, "Yeah." And he pointed to where Bob was sitting in the room.

"And is he wearing sweatpants?"

"Yeah."

Weird, right?

Then someone else got up and said, "You know, I really feel Bob Jones is with us, and I don't know what to do with that."

People aren't trying to make this stuff happen, but when it does—and when we don't know what to do with it—we need to ask God. We need to train our sight to see what heaven is up to. If we believe there is no chasm between life and death, and if people aren't dead in Christ but alive in Christ, then in the *real* reality, we are not communicating with the dead.

And I have a feeling that one of the reasons people from the cloud of witnesses are communicating with us is that they are vibrating with the anticipation of what God is about to release on the earth. They spent their lives sowing into things that are ready for harvest.

Linking back to the question of heaven: if we are to rule with Christ in heaven and continue to advance His Kingdom, is it possible that those who are already "there" and doing that are so excited about it they want to connect with those of us "here" who are also partnering with Christ? Is it possible the cloud of witnesses becomes visible to help us practice seeing the mystical realm…so that we can better see what heaven is doing and help bring it about here on earth? What a feedback loop that would be!

This kind of stuff excites me. But it also makes me nervous because we don't want to get distracted. I don't want to hear that anyone went out and set up a Christian séance and tried to channel their favorite late prophet. I hope you understand that's not what I'm suggesting.

I *am* suggesting that we might be missing out on some of Heaven's messages if we decide that God isn't big enough to communicate from His side of heaven through those who have gone to live with Him. We can keep our hearts open and our discernment on.

DO YOU ACCEPT THE CHALLENGE?

Like I said: I'm "answering" questions with more questions here. I'm not laying out definitive theology. I just want to challenge any cemented thinking we might have developed.

If we invite the Holy Spirit to expand our imagination, we should be prepared to see some extraordinary things—and to go beyond our ordinary understanding.

8: MYSTICAL MISCELLANY

In addition to collecting questions, I've also gathered many notes about the mystical realm over the years. Some of these notes are still stand-alone wonders and ideas, but I think they might be helpful, so I decided to gather some together here.

LOVE

No matter what we're doing—whether it's officially "mystical" or not—we've got to do it with love. As Danny Silk says, "Keep your love on." Heaven's perspective is love, and love is vital if you want to train to see the mystical realm.

WHEN IN DOUBT, CROSSCHECK WITH THE BIBLE

As we grow in our ability to see the unseen, it's helpful to remember that we can't go wrong if there's a solid Bible reference for it.

I was in Florida for a couple of days while writing about angels for my first book. My angel Valor was with me, and he said, "Hey, you should interview me."

And I'm like: "I'm not sure that that's OK. Let me check." So, I asked the Father, and the Father said, "Of course." So I interviewed Valor, and that conversation now forms part of a chapter on angels in *As It Is In Heaven*. That wasn't even controversial because it's not heretical to do stuff that's in the Bible, and there's plenty of biblical precedent for transcribing communication with angels. Daniel did it, and Dr. Luke did it in his account of Gabriel meeting with Mary.

And if the Bible forbids a thing, that's also pretty straightforward. Unless it's not. For example, we're not supposed to be fortune telling or using the stars to dictate our behavior. But the Magi came to see Jesus because of the stars. So, we dive back into Scripture...and we read that the heavens declare His glory. Essentially, the Magi "heard" and saw creation declaring the Messiah.

I should say there that I have had interactions with creation; I have heard creation speak. It was weird. Earlier, I mentioned Romans 8 that creation is alive, and it is groaning. Personally, I don't think that's metaphorical. I think when blood calls out from the ground for justice, that is literal. But I'm not going to look to the stars for signs of what God's saying. I'll do that the old-fashioned way through direct prayer, meditation, and communing with the Holy Spirit.

(A little aside here: I find it interesting that in a Church culture that frowns upon looking at the heavens for signs, we have such fascination with signs in the Heavens! Red moons, eclipses, etc.)

So, if it's in the Bible, we can do it. If the Bible forbids, we don't do it. But then we have the grey area of extra-biblical things. Things that the Bible doesn't mention. Are trances in the bible? Yes. So, should you engage with trances? Sure. Are visions in the Bible? Yes. So, you can engage with visions. Are there cars in the Bible? No. Does that mean we can't drive cars? For things *not* mentioned in the Bible, we use our discernment, and we keep accountable.

LIMINAL SPACES

A liminal space is a space of transformation: the space between what was and what is coming. In liminal spaces, we often sense a spiritual or emotional reaction to the physical place because it has seen so many transformations and passages. Doors are some of the most common liminal spaces. Remember C. S. Lewis, author of *The Chronicles of Narnia?* What is he most famous for? A door at the back of a wardrobe—a portal into somewhere else. That's a great metaphor for a liminal space.

THE UNUTTERABLE

We all love a good story. But sometimes, a story is not to be told. The Apostle Paul wrote that some things were unutterable—things he couldn't share. I'm a little bit—shall I admit?—cynical, when people blog and post every single mystical experience they have. I can't help but wonder: do they have permission? I know that I don't have permission to share everything that I experience or see, and some things are quite simply unutterable.

There is a tension between not sharing every single thing you experience and not having any secrets. I don't think you should have a secret sort of experience that you are ashamed of—that's not what I mean. But similar to personal vs. corporate prophetic words, some things are "for our eyes only." Or at least for a season. And it's up to us to check with Holy Spirit to see what we are at liberty to share.

The Holy Spirit is our comforter and friend. When a friend shares something with us, we are wise to check with him whether or not we have permission to share it—at all or at a later date. For example, when a woman tells a close friend she is pregnant, she often adds whether or not the news is ready to go public. Sometimes, we want to protect the gestation of a word or experience until it is strong enough to grow.

UNEMPLOYED ANGELS

I have encountered angels who weren't currently on assignment, and I call them unemployed angels. Essentially, these angels are unemployed when the person or church they were assigned to decides not to carry out their assignment.

Assignments can be personal or corporate. A church or a ministry often has multiple assignments. Whatever the assignment, there are many reasons people abandon them; they might feel the tasks are too difficult, or they got distracted, or they went down some dead-end streets in their lives. The assignment is still there, but the angel isn't actually *on* assignment; they're waiting for the assignment to be picked up.

Let's keep our angels employed! We need to go after our assignments, not just sit around waiting on angels to do stuff.

Remember: angels aren't here to make things easy. They're here to make things possible.

MANTLES

Angels are also assigned to people with mantles. A mantle is a loose-fitting cloak and also a symbol of covering, authority, and anointing. We get the spiritual concept of the mantle from the story of Elisha, who passed his authority on to Elijah.

A person can have more than one mantle. For example, John Wimber of the Vineyard Church had multiple mantles to birth movements: a worship movement, theological reformation movement, a signs-and-wonders movement, and a church-growth movement.

Once a person receives a mantle, they keep it as long as they are alive. If they pass on without transferring the mantle, it's essentially up for grabs.

As they do with assignments, angels sometimes wait around for someone to pick up a mantle. Mantles are often passed on to spiritual sons and daughters, but those "children" don't always use them. As with abandoned assignments, I think the Church stalls a lot because people are not really interested in wearing the mantle of their spiritual father or mother. That's what happens when you see a lot of activity in a church but nothing is actually being built.

I frequently see rejected and abandoned mantles in the spirit, just hanging in mid-air. To me, they look like emblems or logos. If I enter a church and see a kind of logo in the spirit, it is usually a mantle. I'll try to interpret what it is by asking the Father. Usually, it's meant to be picked up by someone in that church, and I can share that it is available.

TRANCES

I often go into deep trances, especially when receiving prayer during ministry time. And by deep, I mean the kind of trances I don't know if I'm actually going to come out of it.

In some of these trances, God has come to me like a surgeon and started to operate on me and heal my wounds. During one trance, God came to me and held my hands. He started to tell me how He would use my hands as a healing to the nations, prophesying over them about releasing authority through them. Then, I became aware of my physical surroundings and started to "come to." The only thing was, I felt like I was both present and not present. My hands still felt like they were enormous, as they were in the trance. I started telling people around me: "Look! My hands are MASSIVE." I tried getting my car keys from my pocket and I physically couldn't do it because my hands were too big. Over time, the things I have seen in these "unseen" trances have manifested in the seen world. I continue to grow and learn how to interpret them, how to share them, and how to be accountable for them.

As I mentioned earlier, many church leaders were afraid of the prophetic not too long ago. They were afraid to the extent that some churches still refuse to release, train, or deploy a prophetic ministry. However, thanks to a lot of healthy prophets and prophetic ministers, there has been an acceptance of the prophetic. I am hoping that a similar positive shift will happen with the seer ability: that things like trances will be less scary.

A crucial thing for church leaders to understand is that a seer, like a prophet, does not usurp his or her church leadership. When someone has a "word" from God, the word is examined and either rejected, accepted, or waited upon. If the person with the word builds trust with the leader, they also grow in their gift and authority under their leadership.

Similarly, I think we need to start raising up healthy seers who understand that what they see and speak is to be examined and held accountable. It is time for healthy seers to build trust. That will require vulnerability, teachability, and the humility to know that we all get it wrong at times.

DANGERS

As we train our sight, there are a few things to look out for:

Fear

Fear is one of the supreme enemies of engaging with the mystical realm. The Church is so often afraid that the devil has the upper hand. He doesn't. End of story.

Anger

Anger will also hinder our understanding of the mystical realm. When we engage with anger and frustration (frustration is just a nicer way of saying anger), we are giving the enemy permission to control a little bit of our experience of the mystical. We start to resonate with what the devil is doing rather than what heaven is doing.

The Political and Religious Spirit

The political and religious spirits thrive on fear. And if we get sidetracked with either, we're going to mess with our ability to see clearly in the spirit.

These spirits also thrive on division and isolation. We've seen the results throughout history: political parties and church denominations that literally try to kill each other off. No one party or denomination is the answer. The people of God—with all our differences—are the answer. We are *all* the Bride of Christ, and any argument against that is divisive.

What is the central event in all of history? The Cross and Christ crucified. It's *not* the second coming of Christ or our best guess at how His judgment might play out—things the Church spends waaaaaay too much time fighting about. Think how happy the divisive religious spirit is about that! Same for the political spirit. The devil is happy to see you spend your time arguing with someone instead of training your ability to see what heaven is up to.

BLOCKAGES TO SIGHT

Related to dangers are blockages to our spiritual sight. We likely have our own personal blockages, but one of the main blockages to growing in sight and discernment is entertainment. I have never watched a horror movie in my life. Never. Not even the old black-and-white film of Boris Karloff playing *Dracula*. Part of the reason I've never watched scary movies is because they were too real for me as a kid. I already had a vivid imagination; I knew that the dark imagery would stick with me. You might be different but be aware that whatever you put into your imagination will affect this dimmer switch of your perception. When in doubt, check in with the Holy Spirit. If he doesn't give you clearance to watch/participate/experience something, there is a good reason.

NOT EVERYTHING MEANS SOMETHING

One little word of caution: not every single thing you see will mean something. I have a friend whose son sees angels. Once, he watched them picking feathers off of themselves and saying to the rest of the angels, "Wait till you see how they react to this," and they all had a laugh. God (and the angels) have a sense of humor.

Sometimes, when you see the clock reading 11:11, it is a portal into the grace of God for transition. Sometimes it's just eleven minutes past eleven. Sometimes it does mean something, sometimes not. God wants us to keep our eyes on Him…not just on the things He does.

9: FROM GLORY TO GLORY

Every day, we're supposed to be going from Glory to Glory; that means we are to be increasing glory. Are we doing this? Or are we believing any lies that keep us from moving forward on the glory continuum? Are we letting the enemy or a friend detour us from it? Or Fox News, MSNBC, CNN, NPR, the BBC? Are we dividing and diminishing in pessimism, or are we uniting and increasing in hope?

People will divide over anything. It's our job to *unite* in the Kingdom. It's our job to advance the Kingdom of God. It's our job to believe that tomorrow will be better than today because of the increase of God's government and of peace.

There shall be no end to the advancing of the Kingdom. This is such beautiful news! That means we get to continue to grow and learn in the Spirit. We get to expect deeper and deeper encounters with God, the mystical realm, and each other.

We must stay aligned with a Kingdom narrative, not the devil's agenda. Our highest loyalty is to the King—our Father. We are all in a royal bloodline, and we all have responsibilities to carry on the Kingdom work. To do that, we keep our eyes on what the King is doing, and we train to see more clearly.

In the next section, I offer resources to activate your gift to see the mystical realm.

PART TWO

ACTIVATING THE MYSTICAL REALM

ACTIVATION 1: PRAYERS

Good news: if you pray, you already are more mystical than you think.

Think about it: what *is* prayer? "Well," you might say, "prayer is a conversation with God." A conversation actually assumes dialogue, but many of us "converse" with God in a monologue. We do all the talking. And that talking is often whining and complaining and begging. We don't understand prayer because we're actually not engaged with the Spirit realm.

To pray, we need to understand to whom we're praying.

WHAT IS A GOOD FATHER?

Even when we pray to "Our Father" in heaven, we don't always know what a good father is like. We all had different experiences with our natural fathers. For some, a good father was distant but bought you a car when you turned sixteen. For others, a good father didn't beat you—or didn't use a stick when he beat you! And for those like me, a father wasn't really in the picture; mine died when I was 11, and I barely remember him. So this notion of a good father is very subjective.

The secret to prayer is to be in a relationship with the One to whom we are praying—to know His character and His heart. That is how you create and grow a connection between yourself and God. And if you perceive God as distant or punishing, then you have a wonderful discovery of His fatherly love waiting for you.

HOW *NOT* TO PRAY

God loves to give, but He doesn't want to just be loved for what He gives. We reveal the immaturity of our relationship with Him if we're just praying for stuff we want.

Anyone who spends time with young children knows the annoyance of the ask: the "can I…, can I…, can I have…?" When my daughter was two, I had to sneak out to the shoe store to buy myself shoes because she was at the *can I have?* stage, and I didn't want to have to keep saying *no, no, no.*

We ask for things like that as kids. But we shouldn't be asking like that as grownups. Same for our prayer life. Mature prayer is partnership, not begging. We are the Bride of Christ, and the Father is looking for a mature spouse for his Son to marry. When we do make a request of the Father, it should be from a place of healthy relationship.

One of the most misquoted verses in Scripture is Philippians 4:19: "And my God will supply all your needs according to His riches in glory in Christ Jesus" (NASB). Perhaps a better way to think of this scripture would be: God will supply all of your needs because of your generosity.

We can be generous toward God by praying for others. What if we prayed for our pastors' breakthrough? For our local church's breakthrough? For our president's breakthrough—even if you despise whomever is president when you read this (I heard that we're supposed to love our enemies).

As we mature in our seer ability, our prayers will mature, too—and vice versa.

Another thing to avoid is getting all religious about prayer:

> When you pray, you are not to be like the hypocrites; for they love to stand and pray in the synagogues and on the street corners

> so that they may be seen by men. Truly I say to you, they have their reward in full (Matthew 6:5 NASB).

Those who pray publicly to show off are getting their reward then and there—it doesn't go beyond that moment of being seen. But if you're praying in secret, your Father will reward you, and your expectations should be for a reward.

I don't know what that reward is, but it's probably no less than what the guys praying publicly are getting. In the paradox of Spirit, humility is exalted. How do you manage being exalted while being humble? How do you pray in secret while still looking forward to that reward? You do it by being in relationship with the One who gives the reward.

HOW TO PRAY

If our Father knows what we need before we ask Him, how do we pray as seers? How about: "Father, can you show me what *you* know I need? Can you show me how I can partner with what You are doing?"

It starts to feel revolutionary to pray like that. Praying: "God, You know what I need before I've even asked for it" is night-and-day different from praying, "Please, God, I need this thing." If God already knows what we need, and if we believe that and know

He will provide, then part of our prayer can also be thanking Him for what we can't yet see—aka, faith in practice.

When we pray like that, we're making a way for God's plans to happen and reminding ourselves that He is working on our behalf. And when we remember that, we're less likely to rush to make things happen on our own or to make bad decisions.

Jesus said "pray, then, in this way:

> 'Our Father who is in heaven,
> Hallowed be Your name.
> Your kingdom come.
> Your will be done,
> On earth as it is in heaven.
> Give us this day our daily bread.
> And forgive us our debts, as we also have forgiven our debtors.
> And do not lead us into temptation, but deliver us from evil.
> [For Yours is the kingdom and the power and the glory forever. Amen.']" (Matthew 6:9-13 NASB)

Many books and resources break down this prayer into helpful, explanatory sections. I won't do that here. But I do want to emphasize the first part: "Our Father."

Jesus prayed to a good Father. When we're praying, we have to keep in mind that we're not approaching a religious leader or a politician; we don't have to impress or lobby God. We're approaching our Father.

Jesus said that if evil parents know how to give good gifts to their children, how much more will our good, heavenly Father be able to give good gifts to His children?

Does God want you to be wealthy? Let me say as a father: I certainly don't want my children to be on welfare. I want them to learn how to make and build wealth—and I'm not evil! How much more does their heavenly Father want for them? For you?

Only spiritual things are eternal; everything else is temporal. I might want to provide for my children and their children, but that's still not eternal. I want to invest in spiritual things, and I teach my children to do the same. I want them to be able to walk into a room and say, "In Jesus name, I give you what I have." I want them to be able to walk into a room of government in Washington D.C. and proclaim the good news of the Kingdom.

These are the kinds of things I want for my children. And these are the kinds of things our heavenly Father wants for *His* children. For us.

Do we believe He'll come through for us? If not, we need to shift our perception of reality. We need to see beyond the limited, "visible" reality to the limitlessness of heaven.

Following are several prayers I've found helpful in training to see what Heaven is doing:

PRAYER # 1: CHRIST AT THE CENTER

Here is a simple prayer for training in the seer ability:

> Heavenly Father, I pray that You would give me the spirit of wisdom and revelation in the knowledge of Christ. Help me keep Christ at the center of everything I do. Open the eyes of my heart so that I can see in the spirit realm what You want to show me. I ask for dreams, visions, revelations, and visitations. I know that these are a part of my inheritance and the promise of the new covenant. God, I trust that You will enlarge my ability to engage with this mystical realm. Thank You for giving me the wisdom to apply and activate what I see and experience to advance Your Kingdom. In Jesus' name, Amen.

PRAYER #2: SAINT PATRICK'S BREASTPLATE

I love Saint Patrick and his prayer, which is known as either Saint Patrick's Breastplate or The Lorica of Saint Patrick. This mighty prayer is full of power. You can pray all or part of it:

> I arise today
> Through a mighty strength, the invocation of the Trinity,
> Through belief in the Threeness,
> Through confession of the Oneness
> of the Creator of creation.
>
> I arise today
> Through the strength of Christ's birth with His baptism,
> Through the strength of His crucifixion with His burial,
> Through the strength of His resurrection with His ascension,
> Through the strength of His descent for the judgment of doom.
>
> I arise today
> Through the strength of the love of cherubim,

In the obedience of angels,
In the service of archangels,
In the hope of resurrection to meet with reward,
In the prayers of patriarchs,
In the predictions of prophets,
In the preaching of apostles,
In the faith of confessors,
In the innocence of holy virgins,
In the deeds of righteous men.

I arise today, through
The strength of heaven,
The light of the sun,
The radiance of the moon,
The splendor of fire,
The speed of lightning,
The swiftness of wind,
The depth of the sea,
The stability of the earth,
The firmness of rock.

I arise today, through
God's strength to pilot me,
God's might to uphold me,
God's wisdom to guide me,
God's eye to look before me,

God's ear to hear me,
God's word to speak for me,
God's hand to guard me,
God's shield to protect me,
God's host to save me
From snares of devils,
From temptation of vices,
From everyone who shall wish me ill,
afar and near.

I summon today
All these powers between me and those evils,
Against every cruel and merciless power
that may oppose my body and soul,
Against incantations of false prophets,
Against black laws of pagandom,
Against false laws of heretics,
Against craft of idolatry,
Against spells of witches and smiths and wizards,
Against every knowledge that corrupts man's body and soul;
Christ to shield me today
Against poison, against burning,
Against drowning, against wounding,

So that there may come to me an abundance of reward.

Christ with me,
Christ before me,
Christ behind me,
Christ in me,
Christ beneath me,
Christ above me,
Christ on my right,
Christ on my left,
Christ when I lie down,
Christ when I sit down,
Christ when I arise,
Christ in the heart of every man who thinks of me,
Christ in the mouth of everyone who speaks of me,
Christ in every eye that sees me,
Christ in every ear that hears me.

I arise today
Through a mighty strength, the invocation of the Trinity,
Through belief in the Threeness,
Through confession of the Oneness
of the Creator of creation.

PRAYER #3: THE YAHWEH BREATH PRAYER

Both the Greek and Hebrew words for "spirit" mean "breath": Greek is *pneuma* and Hebrew is *ruach*. For this prayer, you are concentrating on your breath to align with your body with your spirit by breathing the name *Yahweh*.

Begin to breathe in and out. Inhale by breathing "Yah" without engaging your vocal chords—just use your breath. Exhale the sound "weh." Keep using your breath to say the name of God, *Yahweh*. Simple. Slow it down—don't hyperventilate.

If your thoughts wander, bring them back to the breath, to the present. God is present with us, right here, right now. By doing this simple prayer, we remind ourselves that we, too are present with Him.

PRAY LIKE YOU'VE GOT THE ANSWER

When we're praying for something and nothing is happening, we tend to pray harder and longer. We're often waiting for God to come to us rather than being aware that He's already with us—right this second. We are already close to God. In fact: what if I told you that you'll never be closer to

God than you are this minute? That we're not waiting on a revival. We *are* revival?

When I got that revelation, I was actually a bit disappointed. And then I got excited to think of what I have access to right this minute. Think of Moses. He was known as the guy who saw God face to face, and yet the Book of Hebrews tells us that we have access to far more glory than Moses did.

The clincher: most of us are just using a fraction of a percent of God's glory. Even if we are walking through the valley of the shadow of death—even if we are walking through shadows of our own making—He is right there with us. God is a good Father, and if we truly believe this, it will change the way we pray. Without knowing the goodness of "Our Father," we are just trying to heft the problems of earth up to heaven instead of bringing heaven to earth.

When we pray like we've already got the answer, we remind ourselves that we do: God *is* the answer. And He's right here with us. And He's working all things for good.

ACTIVATION 2: MEDITATIONS

When most people in the Church hear the word "meditation," they think New Age. It's not. Plus, what we call "New Age" is actually very, very "Old Age." Ancient as the hills, as we'd say in Ireland. But back to meditation: don't worry. The goal of meditation is *not* to get you to empty your mind. The goal is to enter into the heart of the Father. And there are plenty of Scriptures for it; here are two:

> But his delight is in the law of the LORD,
> And in His law he meditates day and night
> (Psalm 1:2 NASB).

> I will meditate on all Your work And muse on Your deeds. (Psalm 77:12 NASB).

The Hebrew word for meditate in those verses is *hagah*. It is the word used to describe the growling of a lion over its prey. Picture the scene; a hungry lion hunts down and kills its next meal. The sense of satisfaction and pleasure is palpable as it hunkers down and begins gnawing at its food. *Hagah* is literally a moaning, murmuring, uttering, and sighing over something.

> "This book of the law shall not depart from your mouth, but you shall meditate on it day and night, so that you may be careful to do according to all that is written in it; for then you will make your way prosperous, and then you will have success" (Joshua 1:8 NASB).

For me, meditating on Scripture is one of the most powerful tools to open the door to the unseen realm. I enjoy activating my imagination with a passage and using my sanctified imagination to picture what was going on and to partner with what the Holy Spirit might reveal to me.

If you've never meditated intentionally, that might sound a bit odd. Before I offer some meditations, here is a bit of helpful advice.

HINDRANCES TO MEDITATION

Have you ever sat down and tried to meditate but then immediately thought, "Did I forget to pick up lettuce for the dinner salad?" And then you try to focus again, "Ah, Jesus..." only to be interrupted by, "Squirrel!" And you ask yourself, "Wait, why am I thinking about squirrels? OK. Focus on Jesus. Meditate." A couple of seconds pass, and then you think, "Wow, I can feel the hairs in my nose right now...."

And it goes on like that until we give up. One way to counter the scroll of clutter that passes through the mind is to keep a notebook and pen by your side as you begin to meditate. Don't beat yourself up for having a stream of thoughts, but write them down; get them out of your head and onto the page. It's a bit like clearing out the rusty pump to get to the clear water.

Then practice breathing. There are many ways to do this. Some people use a mantra, but many Christians freak out at that word. Think of it as a prayer. You might use the Yahweh Breath Prayer. You might say, "Holy, holy, holy." Or you might inhale and pray "Christ within me" then exhale "Christ around me." You might use a favorite Scripture, "Be still, and know that I am God."

Begin to slow down your breath. As you do this, you are calming your body, and those erratic thoughts will begin to subside. If they keep arising, just keep returning your focus to Jesus. Keeping Jesus at the center is the key to meditation. I also believe it's the key to accessing the mystical realm.

Another obstacle to meditating is slipping out of the present. It's so easy to start thinking about the past or the future. Prophetic people can find it especially difficult to be present because they want to hear God for the next thing. But if you can stay in the moment, you will become aware of what the Holy Spirit is doing right this second, and you'll learn to be aligned with the heartbeat of Heaven.

With all of that out of the way, we're ready for the first meditation.

MEDITATION #1: LYING DOWN

For this meditation, you'll be lying down. You already have two times a day when you can easily do this: when you're going to sleep and when you wake up. I like to do this with my eyes open, if only so that I don't fall asleep.

Let's say it's morning. You've just woken up. Stretch out on your back in an intentional recumbent posture, keeping your spine straight. Keep your feet about hip-width apart, and turn your hands so that your palms face up. Be as balanced as you can physically, and keep your whole body still.

Bring your awareness to your feet. Then your ankles. Then your calves. Then your knees…and slowly up through all the main parts of your body until you reach your head. Do this awareness "scan" several times, being fully present and keeping your mind focused on each part of your body as you go.

Then begin to repeat in your mind: *Jesus, You are worthy; Jesus, You are worthy; Jesus, You are worthy*. Think of this as music looping in the background as you continue the rest of this meditation. Now, as you scan up from your feet, begin to bless each part of the body. Bless your feet, bless your ankles, bless your calves, bless your knees….

So far, this has been pretty left-brained and linear. Now you're going to switch to the right brain.

At this point, if you have your eyes closed, open them, but keep your gaze unfocused, softened, as if you're ready to see things in a new way. Remain in that softened state for at least a minute. As you continue to practice, try increasing that time to five minutes. Then ten. Cultivate a sense of surrender to the goodness of God.

Meditation is all about surrender. This is also how you access the heavenly realm: surrendering the grasp you have on earth.

If you do this meditation at night, you can finish by closing your eyes—but still keeping them unfocused. If you fall asleep, what a wonderful way to do it! You'll probably sleep far better after blessing your body and meditating on the goodness of God.

MEDITATION #2: SEATED

This is a seated meditation. It helps to listen to peaceful, wordless music that you enjoy but that does not distract you; be sure it's calm and centering. Find a place to sit—either cross-legged on the floor or in a chair. I like to sit in a comfortable chair so that I can do this meditation without the distraction of my muscles cramping or getting sore. Wherever you sit, keep your back straight, with feet flat on the floor and hip-width apart, one hand on each leg.

Close your eyes. Begin calming down your breathing. You can use the same prayers mentioned in the first meditation, like telling the Lord: "You are worthy, You are worthy." Or use whatever saying or mantra or prayer you like.

As with all the meditations, start by doing a full minute, trying to keep your thoughts focused on Jesus and not running rampant. Then, begin increasing your time until you lose track of time. This can take a while. These days, I almost immediately begin entering another realm. But it took practice, and I continue practicing, because I want to keep growing.

MEDITATION #3: STANDING

This is a standing meditation—and it's my favorite, hands down. Sometimes, when I'm doing this, I remember being a teenager and dancing in my bedroom, hoping no one walked in to see. Basically, I do this one when I'm in the house on my own.

I like to use fifteen lines from the Saint Patrick's Breastplate mentioned in the prayer section. I think of this as a kind of embodied prayer—a meditation spoken with movements of the body.

Here are the lines I use:

> Christ with me,
> Christ before me,
> Christ behind me,
> Christ in me,
> Christ beneath me,
> Christ above me,
> Christ on my right,

Christ on my left
Christ where I lie,
Christ where I sit,
Christ where I arise…

I encourage you to do this when you can engage your body, because it teaches your body to be your body not your mind—as in: reminding the body that it's not in control. St. Patrick started the prayer with this phrase, "I arise today…" So say something along those lines. And then, as you say each of the phrases, engage with the words physically.

Stand up straight and begin with both hands on your heart, and just breathe for about thirty seconds.

Say, "I arise today," and then:

Christ with me (wrap your arms around yourself)
Christ before me (lift your arms out in front of you)
Christ behind me (gently swing your arms behind you)
Christ in me (reach your arms out and up, drawing them toward yourself)
Christ beneath me (reach down to your feet)

> Christ above me (reach up above your head)
> Christ on my right (twist your body to the right)
> Christ on my left (twist your body to the left)
> Christ where I lie (lie down)
> Christ where I sit (sit up)
> Christ where I arise (finish by standing)

You can continue to slowly repeat the words and actions for several minutes, up to ten. Keep your eyes closed, and allow your imagination to wander in heavenly ways and places.

When you're done, notice how you feel. Are you more aware of the mystical realm around you? Have you slowed down the mind chatter? Are you more aware of the presence of the Holy Spirit? Of the mystical realm? This active meditation builds your awareness that Christ is with you, within you, and around you. You are centered in Him. When I practice this prayer, it's like I've entered the embrace of Christ.

MEDITATION #4: WALKING

So, we've had a lying, a seated, and a standing meditation. And now for a walking meditation. By the time you start to do this, you should be able to get into the zone reasonably quickly. I enjoy doing this in the mountains, but you can do it while walking anywhere. You really just need a little space—in fact, if it's raining cats and dogs, you can walk in circles in your living room.

This meditation is about slowing everything down. As with all the other meditations, you start by getting quiet, by focusing on your breathing, and by praying a word or phrase to focus your mind. You might use the word "Yahweh" and do the Yahweh Breath Prayer—or anything that resonates with you.

I often walk with one or both hands on my heart. I consider the heart to be the very core of who we are body, soul, spirit. So, I like to keep my hands on my heart because where you're focused is where the energy goes. I am not one of those who believes that the Biblical principle of laying of hands is symbolic. It is a transference of something wonderful and mystical, a God given impartation. I choose to lay hands of my heart, or my stomach, or my lower abdomen as a way of imparting strength to my gut feelings or my heart health.

As with any other meditations, the minute a distracting thought enters your mind, just refocus on Jesus. You can also train yourself to do that by choosing a body part to focus on as a reminder to refocus, like your hands.

Walk for 5, 10, 15, 30 minutes. You will experience a shift in your heart. When you do, begin to use your faith to see in the mystical realm. Begin to see with the eyes of your heart—ask God to open the eyes of your heart.

Begin to pray like you are seated with Christ in Heaven—as you are! And from there, you can pray from heaven to earth.

THE PLEASURE OF MEDITATION

Practice doesn't make perfect, but it does make you better at something. Practice engrains a habit, even when it's hard. The first week or two back at the gym can be pretty tough, but by returning daily and by doing the reps, we get better and stronger. It is the same with meditation. Just start with one meditation a day for a few minutes. Be consistent. As you continue to meditate on God, you'll increase your awareness of His Kingdom and of the other dimensions around you.

And it's hard to go wrong when you meditate on the truth of Scripture. Remember: Joshua 1:8 says the book of the law shall not depart from your mouth, but you shall meditate on it (gnaw at it) day and night. We chew at Scripture, we suck out and savor every little piece of satisfaction and nourishment we can. The best food is both, good tasting and good for us. Health and pleasure don't have to be mutually exclusive.

In fact, here's a thought: meditation is not about trying to deny all of our desires. I fundamentally believe we were created for pleasure. I realize that goes against every austere teaching that the Church has adopted over the years. But think of it: what if we were created for pleasure? If I invited you to a garden of pleasure, you would think I'd gone hedonistic? But that's what *Eden* means. We're supposed to be restoring this garden of pleasure. We're supposed to take pleasure in the Lord and in being together.

Meditation should be pleasurable. Each time we finish a session of meditation, we have the chance to feel even more loved by God and to love Him even more. May your meditations be full of joy in His presence.

ACTIVATION 3: ENCOUNTERS

By definition, an encounter is a meeting. But when we encounter God, we aren't just meeting, we are experiencing a new depth of His love and beauty. Whether you initiate it or God does, an encounter will leave you changed for the better.

Bonus: the more we encounter God's love and goodness, the more excited we are to share it with others.

ENGAGING THE IMAGINATION FOR ENCOUNTERS

Scripture is a great way to begin an encounter. One of my favorite passages for igniting my imagination and encountering God is Psalms 118. If you haven't read it recently, do; it is rich with goodness. I'll just give you a teaser here with verse 14:

> The LORD is my strength and song,
> And He has become my salvation (NASB).

That verse quotes a song in Exodus 15:2 sung by Moses and the Israelites after the Lord had saved them from Pharaoh. That same song was also likely sung after the foundations of the Temple had been rebuilt in Ezra Chapter 3. Jesus quoted this song. It was quoted during His triumphal entry into Jerusalem on Palm Sunday. And it may have been the song Jesus and His disciples sang directly after the Last Supper as they made their way to the Mount of Olives.

What a Scripture to ignite the imagination!

When I read this song, I begin to imagine what David was thinking about when he wrote it. He wrote from a place of remembrance activated by his God-given imagination. I wonder: did he picture all those moments when God rescued him? Was he recalling all the times he experienced the goodness of God, the forgiveness, the mercy? When he wrote about the Lord being his strength and his song, was he remembering singing songs of triumph before battles? Was he thinking of the strength he had when facing down the giant? Did he ever imagine how and where his song might someday be sung? Did he have any idea that Jesus would one day sing it?

Then I let my imagination go to Jesus. Generations later, when Jesus was about to suffer more than any man had, He sang David's song of triumph and victory. Was He thinking of all the times He stood beside David in *his* suffering? Was He looking forward to seeing David in heaven? Was He wondering what that meeting would look like—how would David feel and react when he finally saw the face of his Shepherd?

Then I remember the Mount of Olives and imagine what Jesus thought of meeting all the Old Testament saints. That was the joy set before him. For *that* joy, Jesus endured the Cross. Of course, He had met the saints already, but all those saints were about to meet Him and be reconciled. Abraham, Moses, Rahab, Esther—imagine what it was like when they saw Jesus!

Then I start to remember the goodness of God in my own life. I start to remember how God has rescued me—time and time again. How He has brought me to a place of abundance. And then I imagine meeting *Him*, face to face. And then it's back to the Verse-1 gratitude that started it all off:

> Give thanks to the LORD, for He is good;
> For His loving kindness is everlasting (Psalms 118:1 NASB).

The Bible is bursting with verses that can ignite our imagination, but encounters can happen with anything, any time. You can have an encounter with God at your kitchen table waiting for the coffee to brew. You can go to a great big gathering and experience a guided encounter. However you do it, just do it. Encountering God is a great way to strengthen your seer ability.

Over the years, I've been pursuing people who can teach me what I don't already know, which is a lot. I heard about a man who gets up in the morning and practices going into the Spirit. He imagines getting into an elevator and the doors closing. He goes down and down. And when the doors open, some scene will be spread before him—different every time.

I started doing this, and I love it. And after a while it became normal. As we normalize and activate our seer ability, we will see more of the mystical realm.

Here are a few encounters to get you going. Use them as starting points to create your own encounters.

ENCOUNTER #1: PERMISSION TO SEE

This is a helpful starter encounter—especially if you are hesitant about the whole idea. You can do this anywhere you won't be interrupted. If you like, put on some music you love—something that reminds you of God's love. Get comfortable—maybe sit in a favorite chair or lie on the floor.

Grant yourself permission to start to imagine what it's like to interact with the unseen. Read this over yourself:

> Father, I love to rest in Your arms. From that place of safe embrace, I would like to practice seeing with Your eyes—with the eyes of heaven. I would like to see Your angels and be reminded of the ways they carry out Your work.

And then:

1. Be still.

2. Remembering the power in our tongues, speak a truth, like a Scripture.

3. Speak this over yourself: *I give myself permission to dream while awake. I give myself permission to use my imagination to access the mystical realm. Father I thank You for giving me the ability to see. Thank You that I can see the unseen. I just pray in Jesus' name that there will be no deception. Help me be free to see what You are doing.*

4. And then, close your eyes to see....

ENCOUNTER #2: OPENING THE IMAGINATION WITH SCRIPTURE

One of the easiest ways to start intentionally having encounters is via Scripture. You can use a Scripture you already love, or you can use Psalm 118 and open your imagination like I described at the start of this chapter. Another good place to start is Psalm 46:10: "Be still, and know that I am God" (NIV). This verse has become the way I quiet myself before Him—in prayer, meditation, and encounter.

This encounter sounds pretty simple: choose a small passage of Scripture and read it a few times, slowly. Let it soak in. Open your imagination. Invite the Holy Spirit to speak to you. Ask questions. Engage your sense of wonder. You can experience more of Him than you ever thought imaginable.

ENCOUNTER #3: JOY, LOVE, & PEACE

This encounter is a tool that helps train our imagination to practice good thoughts and feelings. Here's the thing: when we think negative thoughts, we're using our imaginations to create and rehearse negative realities. What if we rehearsed—imagined—good things? Like the feelings of love, joy, and peace. It's hard to go wrong with the fruit of the Spirit! And if we practice, it can even become easy to start aligning our feelings with those positive realities.

This encounter is also helpful when you face something externally negative. For example, when I discover I'm listed on another heresy watch list, I could let my thoughts spiral into despair—or I could meditate on Philippians 4:8:

> [W]hatever is true, whatever is noble, whatever is right, whatever is pure, whatever is lovely, whatever is admirable—If anything is excellent or praiseworthy—think about such things (NIV).

So pick one: love, peace, or joy. I'll use joy as an example here. Think of a time you felt joy. If you haven't felt joy in a while, think back to a time in your childhood. Even if you had a rough childhood, moments of joy are often far more memorable when we are young. It could be something as simple as being at school and hearing the recess bell. Or if recess wasn't pleasurable for you, think of the moment the end-of-day school bell rang. Or when you received a Christmas gift you'd been dreaming of. Find a moment of joy you remember, and cultivate that feeling.

Begin feeling sensations in your body. What does joy feel like on your face? What if you smile while trying to notice? And your neck: if your neck is often tensed in tense situations, what if you spoke joy to your neck and let it relax? You can align the feelings of your physical body to your emotional feelings. And if you get distracted, speak or think the word "joy." Invite joy into your spirit, mind, and body. If it feels weird, speak the words of Philippians 4:8 again.

You'll find your own way to cultivate the good feeling, and you can do it for joy, love, and peace—and other good things. Then start rehearsing what it will look like when you're the most joyful, most loving, most peaceful person on the planet.

You can do this in silence or listening to wordless, calming music. You can do it while sitting or lying down. Take five, full moments. If you can, build up to more.

Afterward: do you feel more joy? More peace? More love? Did you struggle to stick with positive thoughts? This is definitely a discipline that requires training. But can you imagine what would happen if we all did this every day? We would literally change our genetic structure; we would activate dormant genes that get bombarded by our negative thoughts all day long.

A warning here: if you approach the mystical realm as a victim, this won't work. If you're not the agent of your own emotional health and wellbeing, and if you're waiting on external things to change your wellbeing, then you are a victim. If I need something to change for me to feel better, I have become a victim. If I need you to be different for me to be different, I have become a codependent victim. This is emotional health 101, but I've mentioned it several times in this book because it can be so easily overlooked. And if, when you try to activate your imagination, you find yourself in a victim role, that's a great opportunity to forgive and heal.

Another reminder: this unseen, mystical realm is an exercise in faith. And faith is a substance of things hoped for. All real things have substance: energy and matter. Faith is a real thing, and all of life is turned on by faith. So just because you don't *feel* joy doesn't mean you don't have it. Just because you don't *feel* faith, doesn't mean it doesn't exist. When we activate these realities in our lives, our feelings will begin to align with those realities.

The mystical realm will always be activated by faith. We increase our potential to enter into the mystical realm when we can exercise and train our faith to see it. And one of the ways to grow our faith is to honor the measure of faith we've been given already. That means we don't discount the little steps, the small victories—even if that's just one, full minute of feeling joy. Cultivate and celebrate what you have, and also ask God for more. He loves to give us more.

ENCOUNTER #4: CREATE YOUR OWN

You've got the tools. You've got the redeemed imagination. Now go for it!

CONCLUSION

Behold, I stand at the door and knock; if anyone hears My voice and opens the door, I will come in to him and will dine with him, and he with Me.

—Revelation 3:20, NIV

This verse is an invitation to intimacy with Jesus. If we want to grow in our ability to see and discern, we must grow in intimacy with Jesus. If we have problems with intimacy—with God or humans—we will have problems with seeing.

People, usually men, often tell me that they have a hard time connecting with God during worship. Interestingly, these men have no issues connecting with their emotions at a sporting event. But in worship? Not so much. I always ask them, "Do you connect intimately with anyone in your life?" Sometimes they will say they can connect with their spouse, but nine times out of ten, they struggle to connect with anyone intimately.

Intimacy is vital if you want to grow in the seer gift and discernment, so whatever blockages you may have, get them fixed. Get inner healing, deliverance, or therapy but learn to open your life to people. Jesus made us both whole and holy on the Cross, but sometimes we need to contend for what He has already given us.

BUILD YOUR TRUST

The thought of seeing in the spirit realm might make you afraid. If you had nightmares or saw monsters in your room as a child, you may have switched off your dimmer switch to protect yourself.

We might want more of the seer gift, but we want it sanitized. Remember: if our earthly fathers do not give us a stone when we ask for bread, how much more will our heavenly Father give good gifts to those who ask? Trust Him. Seeing and discernment are good gifts—gifts that we should eagerly seek while trusting that He who gives the gift will also help us grow in the ability to use it well.

BE IN COMMUNITY & GROW IN DISCERNMENT

Learning to see is not a race. It's also not a one-man show; we need to be surrounded by a faith-filled people who will give us honest feedback. We need a community that does not just echo what we want to hear.

Part of building a healthy faith grid is running alongside powerful people who desire for you to be better, stronger, and more powerful. There is a difference between getting feedback from someone who thinks everything you do smells fishy and someone who loves you, supports you, and prays for greater influence and favor on your life. That is particularly true when you surround yourself with other discerners.

We must grow our discernment to maturity. We must let go of the suspicion and judgment we have used to distance ourselves from other people and other churches. Discernment's time has come.

UNDERSTAND THE KINGDOM

To grow in any gift of the Spirit, we need a healthy understanding of the Kingdom. We don't have to wait around for Jesus to do something else to inaugurate His Kingdom on earth as it is in heaven. He did not ask us to pray for something unattainable or that only happens when He comes again. We are told that the Kingdom is at hand. In fact, the Kingdom is within us.

It is the Father's good pleasure to give us the Kingdom. He even gives us a definition of the Kingdom; it is righteousness, peace, and joy in the Holy Spirit—the very Spirit who gives these gifts to us.

Many people are waiting until they get to heaven so they can be with Jesus. But He is already living inside of us by His Spirit. The issue for us is not proximity—it is awareness. When we cultivate an awareness of the Spirit and His mission to make earth like heaven, we gain access to the unseen realm, and we are encouraged to advance the Kingdom of God right here, right now.

This Kingdom runs on faith, hope, and love—and the greatest is love. So even if we see what the enemy is doing, we can discern and see what God is doing. And He is always moving in love.

God's Kingdom is also victorious; this has to be the foundation for our understanding of the Kingdom. We *must* have a victorious mindset when we consider God's vision for this world.

The problem with the unexamined progress of humanity is that it is generally aimless and visionless. We won't define our destination if we've accepted on some deep level that it has been defined for us and we are just chugging away on a fixed railroad track of destiny.

I think of these lines from *The Vision of the Godhead:*

> Unchanging and Unchangeable, before angelic eyes,
> The Vision of the Godhead in its tranquil beauty lies...
>
> —Frederick William Faber

I want to suggest that the end—the destination—has never changed. We might get there through many changing ways, but the unchanging goal is the Kingdom of God.

For any Kingdom to exist, it must have four components: a monarch, his/her subjects, a territory, and rules. Jesus is our monarch, our King. He is not waiting to become King of heaven and earth; He has already been crowned and currently sits at the right hand of the Father. We, the Church, are His subjects. Earth is His territory. And the rules are to love God, our neighbors, and ourselves. And while we're at it, destroy the works of the devil.

I believe that a proper expectation of an advancing Kingdom composed of His righteousness, His peace, and His joy will help us grow in discernment and seeing.

RECEIVE OTHER SEERS

Thank you for reading this book. You have sown into my life and honored the call God has placed on me. My prayer is that you receive a reward for doing this. Scripture tells us that if we receive a prophet as a prophet, we will receive a prophet's reward. When we acknowledge a person and his gift, we position ourselves to receive what he carries. That is why I sent the first honorarium I ever received to people I admire; I wanted to receive what they carry. I sent the first check I received from selling my first book—even before I had recouped my costs—to a leader I greatly admire because I wanted to honor who she is and receive what she carries.

Sowing into someone, above and beyond what you give to the Church, creates a space for you to receive something from them. If nothing else, it opens your heart toward them and their message. May the time you've sown into my ministry by reading this multiply in your seer journey.

And most importantly, may this book help you grow in your love for Jesus. There is simply nobody like Jesus.

> Father, thank you for inviting us to see You. I ask for even more sight and for a greater awareness of the open Heaven over our lives—a greater awareness of all that You are doing in us. I pray that we would grow in our understanding of the mystical realm to better partner with You to advance Your Kingdom. I pray that we would train to

carry out our assignments, fully committed to seeing all that You are doing in our lives, in our families, in our workplaces, in our churches, in our businesses, in our cities, in our regions, and in our nation. God, help us be aware of what heaven's doing. Help us to see and discern Your work, free of any limiting hindrance. Open our eyes and the eyes of our hearts that we would see Who is for us and not worry about who's against us. Bless us and keep us. Shine Your face upon us and give us peace. Amen.